# Off-Road Driving Techniques

**Nick Dimbleby**

# Off-Road Driving Techniques

The Crowood Press

First published in 1997 by
The Crowood Press Ltd
Ramsbury, Marlborough
Wiltshire SN8 2HR

**British Library Cataloguing in Publication Data**

A catalogue record for this book is available from the British Library.

ISBN 1 86126 052 0

All reasonable care has been taken with the research, compilation and writing of this book.
However, the author, editor and publisher cannot be held responsible for errors or omissions
therein. We must therefore point out that readers are entirely responsible for their own
actions and safety. Off-roading can be dangerous – take care!

Typeset by Phoenix Typesetting, Ilkley, West Yorkshire.
Printed and bound in Great Britain by the Bath Press.

# Contents

# Acknowledgements

A large number of people have assisted in the writing of this book, both directly and indirectly, and I hope that you will permit me to thank them all.

'Thank yous' firstly to off-roading gurus David Bowyer, Keith Hart, David Mitchell and Ronnie Dale, who afforded me my first proper lessons in off-roading through a series about off-road driving schools I did with Gary Pusey, whom I also thank for the experience.

The staff at *Land Rover Owner* (Carl Rodgerson, Simon Huber and Margaret Wey) and *International Off-Roader* (Richard and Cathie Howell-Thomas and Colin Dawson) deserve a credit for allowing me to indulge my passion in print and for liberating many of my photographs for use in this book.

Thanks also to: Peter and Marian Taylor and Jim and Mary Moulter for organizing a couple of superb off-road expeditions in the States; John Cockburn for teaching more about off-road racing in a weekend than most people would learn in a year; and Cristophe Chevalet of *4˜4 magazine*, France, for his continuing enthusiasm, encouragement and expertise.

From Camel Trophy I should like to thank: Lee Farrant, Nick Horne, Karl Trunk, Nigel Quilter, Bob and Joe Ives, Marc Day, Will Tapley, John Leach and Fiona Harbottle. Thanks also to Roger Crathorne and the rest of the team at the Land Rover Experience school.

I should also like to thank numerous individuals from 4˜4 manufacturers: Bill Baker, Denis Chick, Simon Maris, Nick Argent from Land Rover UK; Jennifer O'Brien, Bob Burns and Rob Walsh from Land Rover North America; Jean-Philippe Coulaud and David Barrière from Rover France; Peter Rawlinson, Tom Johnston and Mervyn Aisles from Chrysler Jeep; James Thomas and Lynda Shewan from Toyota; Phil Harwood, Austin Craig and Alan Denton at Vauxhall; Andy Kirk at Lada; and Tony Petit and Trina Brindley at Goodyear.

As for off-roading companions, I have shared many superb trips with: Andy Blois, David Lane, James Rudd, the late Tim Webster, Tony Cable, Ivan Kendle, David Morgan, Larry Byrne, Dominic Marder, Debbie Fletcher, Frank Elson and David Knight – long may they continue! Seasoned off-roader Craig Pusey deserves special mention for being such an erstwhile companion on more trips than I care to remember.

Finally I should like to thank my publishers at the Crowood Press. Their patience has been legendary!

Nick Dimbleby, London, 1997

# 1 Introduction – General Points and Environmental Concerns

Over the past few years there has been a tremendous increase in the sales of 4x4 vehicles, with virtually every major car manufacturer having at least one off-roader in its line up. Whereas the 1980s was the decade of the Volkswagen Golf GTi or 16 valve hot hatch, the fashionable transport of the 1990s seems to be the 4x4 or off-road leisure vehicle, with the Land Rover Discovery and Mitsubishi Shogun market leaders in the UK.

Despite the fact that these vehicles and most modern 4x4s are excellent performers off the tarmac it has been calculated that only 5 per cent of these new vehicles will ever be used off-road. The furthest away from the

*Fig.1 A Discovery owner doing what only five per cent of 4x4 owners do – taking it off-road.*

*Fig.2 With a bit of knowledge, any off-road vehicle can be a passport to adventure.*

how to change gear. But driving off-road legally, safely and successfully requires much more know-how than just pointing your vehicle at the nearest muddy field and setting off in the low-ratio gears. Indeed, off-road driving is so different from day-to-day tarmac motoring that it is almost advisable to forget everything that your driving instructor taught you all those years ago!

Without intending to sound facetious or over-academic, off-road driving could be described as an art. Successful and safe off-roading is not something that you can 'pick up' in an afternoon, and you should never overestimate your own abilities or those of your vehicle. An experienced off-road driver will be able to make an ill-equipped off-roader perform excellently in the mud, just as an inexperienced one can make a meal of an obstacle in a well-prepared and suitably equipped 4x4. It's simply a case of appreciating your own limitations (and those of the vehicle) and adapting your driving style appropriately.

## BE AWARE

As you become more and more familiar with driving off-road, you will realize that you are making much more use of your senses than you would do perhaps on-road. To avoid becoming stuck for example, you have to be constantly aware of the ground conditions ahead of you, as well as reacting to those in which you are traversing. The former can be judged by looking beyond your immediate field of vision, while the latter relies on you correctly assessing the feedback given to you by the vehicle.

Successful off-roading relies very much on the 'feel' of the vehicle; something that you will come to appreciate as you drive more and more off-road. It is therefore vitally important that you are 100 per cent familiar

tarmac most drivers venture is one wheel on the pavement outside the local patisserie while the owner pops in to buy a bagful of brioches.

However, as ownership of a 4x4 becomes less of a fashion statement, more and more owners are expressing a desire to use their vehicles for what they were truly intended. The same vehicle used as a shopping trolley during the week can be a passport to adventure come the weekend.

A great deal of the marketing rhetoric used by major 4x4 manufacturers plays upon this freedom and adventure image, to the extent that many people think that all they need to go off-roading is a vehicle and a knowledge of

*Fig.3 When driving off-road you will be making much more use of your senses. Make sure that you are 100 per cent familiar with your vehicle.*

with your vehicle and its controls. Knowing when to increase the throttle; when to grip the steering wheel lightly and let ruts guide you; or when to back right off is something that you can only learn by trial and error. You can't beat experience when off-roading, and no book – however good it may be – can teach you everything. It is therefore suggested that you use this volume as a lesson and reference for correct off-road driving techniques.

## THE DANGERS

If you are a beginner, it is important to realize how potentially dangerous off-

roading can be. Unfortunately you cannot become an expert overnight, so don't try to attempt the impossible unless you are confident enough to know what to do if things go wrong. Similarly, just because someone else has successfully driven up a hill or sped through a mud run without getting stuck, it doesn't necessarily mean that you too will be able to do it. The other driver may have more experience than you, or their vehicle could be better equipped. If ever you are in doubt or feel as though something is unsafe, don't do it!

If you are new to off-roading you will find that driving off-road is very different from your on-road mileage. For example, your average speeds off-road are likely to be a

*Fig.4 Off-road driving can be dangerous. A moment's loss of concentration and this can happen . . .*

*Fig.5 Driving too fast when off-road is hazardous – you must remember to drive within the limitations of the vehicle and track.*

tenth of your speed on tarmac, while you will probably be making much more use of the vehicle's gears and less of the brake. Engine braking is your main friend off-road, so you should never be coasting out of gear while the vehicle is in motion – as you shouldn't on tarmac. Your vehicle's low-range gearbox (see Chapter 2) should be used for most off-road situations, and four-wheel drive should always be selected.

Travelling in low range will seem terribly slow at first, and there are certain peculiarities associated with this lower ratio when compared to on-road use. For example, it is rare that you will need to pull off in first gear when low range is selected – the gearing

ratio is just too short. Your top gear in low range is unlikely to give you a comfortable speed in excess of 35 mph, so you will find that you will be travelling at a slower speed than this in most cases. Off-road guru David Bowyer has coined a phrase to describe the ideal speed for off-roading: 'As slowly as possible and as fast as necessary'. In other words, take your time when driving off-road. If you need to use momentum to get through or up an obstacle then don't be shy, but at the same time don't overdo it unnecessarily.

As you progress through this book, you will find that some of the techniques that are useful for one area can equally be applied to another. For example, rocking the steering

*Fig.6 At all times be aware of the capabilities of your vehicle. Some obstacles are just too technical.*

wheel from side to side in a see-saw motion causes the front tyre lugs to bite into the ground, and this will often help you keep moving when a less 'aggressive' attitude would result in the vehicle becoming stuck. This technique can be used for mud, hill-climbing, sandy terrain and snow.

Likewise you will find that there are sometimes several different techniques (or at least varying methods) according to what vehicle you are driving. The most obvious of these are the differing 'rules' for automatic and manual gearboxes, while your vehicle's four-wheel drive system can be one of three alternatives. Similarly, expensive bodywork and longer rear overhangs will limit the off-road potential of certain off-road vehicles and you should be sensitive to this.

Apart from this, there is no reason why a brand new top-of-the-range Range Rover 4.6 HSE should not be any less (or more!) capable than a 30-year-old Series II Land Rover. Once again, successfull and safe off-roading is just a case of being aware of your capabilities and those of your vehicle. If you keep reminding yourself of this while you are off-road then you won't go far wrong.

## SUCCESSFUL OFF-ROADING AND COMMON SENSE

When driving off-road you should have three key objectives in mind: i) everything that you

*Fig.7 The author broke the rules by off-roading alone and paid the price – £1,000 worth of damage and wounded pride.*

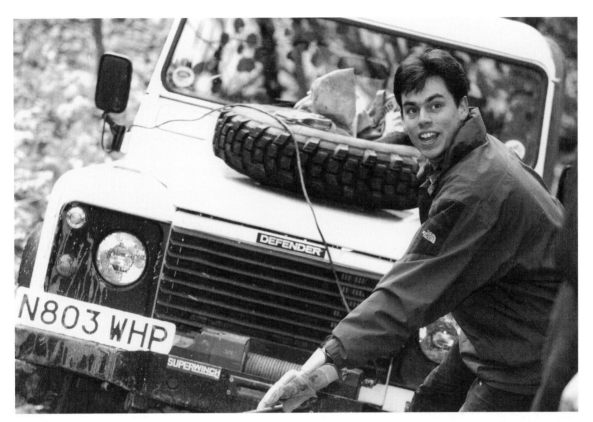

*Fig.8 A vehicle-mounted electric winch is a useful accessory as it allows you to recover yourself from virtually any situation.*

do should be safe and not cause damage to the vehicle; ii) you should not stray from legal rights of way and cause damage to the terrain; and iii) you should keep going and avoid getting stuck.

Naturally becoming stuck should be the least of your worries, but by the same token it is highly advisable to have a second vehicle with you to assist with recovery should you cease forward motion or break down. In short you should never go off-roading alone, as the author learnt when he became stuck in a tricky water section on a green lane in Surrey. Fortunately he was able to summon assistance on a mobile phone, but by the time a friend arrived in another 4x4 some ninety minutes later, water had leaked in through the door seals of the vehicle on test causing

over £1,000-worth of damage to the carpets and interior. In this case, becoming stuck was a major worry!

One exception to the 'never off-road alone' rule is if your vehicle is fitted with a front or rear-mounted winch. The winch is a lifeline for self-recovery, and providing there is an anchor or tree on which to connect up to you can pretty much pull your vehicle out of (or up) anything. A winch is also a useful insurance policy to have if you are off-roading in a group, and its ability to allow continued forward motion where all traction is lost will allow you to tackle more difficult tracks as you become more proficient.

Although a winch is a nice 'luxury' item, there is a minimum list of equipment that you must always take with you when off-roading.

*Fig.9 A small convoy of vehicles off-roading on an ancient byway in the Lake District. By 'treading lightly', these off-roaders are preserving these tracks for the enjoyment of others.*

Some of these items are for vehicle recovery should you become stuck (this list is outlined in Chapter 3), while others are more general items that are for your own comfort and safety. Even though you might not think it necessary to take a sleeping bag and some extra food for an off-road trip in the UK, such items are a useful insurance policy should things go seriously wrong. You may also like to consider taking a mobile phone with you if you have one, although you should be aware that many remote areas of the UK may not be covered by service.

As with any type of outdoor activity, make sure that someone else knows where you are going and what time you expect to return. At all times be prepared for the worst, with enough food and water to last you for at least a day, and some extra warm clothing just in case it becomes colder than you expected. The really prepared off-roader always has a complete change of clothes, just in case the ones they started off in become muddy or soaked during the day's proceedings!

## TREAD LIGHTLY!

The popularity of off-road driving has an effect on the environment, so it is imperative that all off-roaders are aware of the Tread Lightly! programme that has now spread worldwide after originally being set up in the USA.

Tread Lightly! isn't just a phrase, it is a non-profit organization run in conjunction with the US Forest Service and Bureau of Land Management with support from all the major 4x4 manufacturers and importers in the US. Established in 1990, Tread Lightly!'s principal aim is to promote safe and non-damaging multiple use of public lands. All members pledge to use – and not to abuse – the environment.

The principles of the Tread Lightly! programme are summarized with the mnemonic 'T-R-E-A-D':

- Travel only where motorized vehicles are permitted. Never blaze your own trail.
- Respect the rights of ramblers, bikers, campers and others to enjoy their activities undisturbed. Loud motors and noisy behaviour are not acceptable and detract from a quiet outdoor setting. Be especially cautious around horses or ramblers – pull off to the side of the track, switch off your engine and let them pass.
- Educate yourself by obtaining travel maps

*Fig.10 Always 'Tread Lightly'! Sticking to established routes is important wherever you may travel.*

and regulations from public agencies, complying with signs and barriers and asking owners' permission to cross private property. Honour all gates, fences and barriers that are there to protect the natural resources. If you have to open a gate that is shut, make sure that you close it again once you have passed through.

- Avoid streams, lakeshores, meadows, muddy roads and trails, steep hillsides, wildlife and livestock. Driving in wet and boggy areas can cause deep ruts that may result in long-term scarring. Creating ruts in an area with a high water table may cause excess erosion when water diverts into the ruts and erodes the ground still further.
- Drive responsibly to protect the environ-

ment and preserve opportunities to enjoy your vehicle on wild lands. Remember the reasons why you are driving in the country in the first place. If it is to get away from it all, then bear in mind that others may also be there to find peace and solitude themselves.

Although the Tread Lightly! programme originates from the United States, the points made above are just as applicable elsewhere. It is imperative when off-roading on public land (such as green lanes and all other vehicular rights of way) to have respect for the terrain and also for other users. Do not just blast your way through tricky sections; instead, figure the best way through. If you feel that it would be difficult to drive without

*Fig.11 Take care when off-roading, and only attempt something like this when you're experienced enough to get yourself out of trouble!*

causing significant environmental damage, turn around and leave it for another day. Likewise, if there is a tricky section or obstacle that can be avoided by going via another route, do so. Sensible off-roaders always take the easiest option, which is normally the one that leaves the least impact on the land. Why put yourself and your vehicle at risk when there's a perfectly good alternative nearby ?

# 2  What is an Off-Road Vehicle?

Park an off-road vehicle next to a 'normal' family saloon, and it only takes a quick glance to see that they are radically different. Although some saloons (the Subaru range or the Audi Quattro series for example) feature permanent four-wheel drive, off-roaders feature higher ground clearance, the possibility to fit larger tyres, minimal front and rear overhangs and a longer travel suspension system to soak up the bumps.

Of course, some off-road vehicles are better suited to extreme conditions than others, and each vehicle has its particular advantages and disadvantages, especially if road use is taken into account. For example, the Land Rover Defender 90 has minimal overhangs, permanent four-wheel drive and easy-to-repair aluminium bodywork – all of which are useful for difficult off-road tracks – but it may not be as comfortable to drive on-road as, say, a Toyota RAV4. The RAV4, on the other hand, does not feature a transfer box to reduce the vehicle's gearing (see below), and this can make negotiating tricky off-road routes difficult.

As well as being imperative for off-roading, four-wheel drive can also be advantageous on-road. With all four wheels being driven, roadholding and handling is vastly improved – in a sense you have the advantages of front-wheel drive and rear-wheel drive in one neat package. You've only got to look at the enormous success of the Audi Quattros in the World Rally Series during the early 1980s to see the benefits of permanent four-wheel drive in all circumstances.

*Fig.12 Try doing this in any normal family saloon . . .*

Where the Quattro really scored was in its ability to put power down on loose or slippery surfaces. Two-wheel drive rally cars would be sliding about all over the place, but the Quattro would remain easy to handle thanks to its full-time four-wheel drive system.

However, away from flat slippery surfaces it's a very different story: for example, a Range Rover fitted with road tyres will have virtually no advantage over an Audi Quattro saloon on a forest track or on a flat field. However, should the field be heavily rutted or very bumpy, then the Range Rover's long travel suspension and higher ground clearance will allow it to negotiate humps and ruts with ease, while the Audi would very likely become grounded. It's simply a case of putting the traction you have into contact with the ground.

It is for this reason that off-road vehicles sit higher up off the ground than normal saloons. Extra space is required for the longer travel suspension systems demanded by the need to cross undulating terrain, while the bodywork also needs to be higher than

normal to prevent grounding and/or damage in extreme off-road situations. Long travel suspension results in excellent axle articulation, which will help keep all four wheels on the ground for maximum traction.

Off-road vehicles are also structurally different from saloons (with one or two exceptions), featuring a separate chassis and body as opposed to the more common monocoque structure synonymous with road-going cars. A separate chassis offers additional rigidity and strength for the rigours of off-roading, while a lightweight body coupled with a heavy chassis gives a low centre of gravity that is useful for traversing side slopes. A simple and easy to maintain mechanical arrangement is also beneficial, and some designs – such as the Land Rover Defender – take this one step further by

*Fig.13 Most off-road vehicles feature longer travel suspension systems to keep all four wheels on the ground in the most extreme situations.*

having body panels that are easy to remove and replace. This is one reason why Land Rovers have been so popular with military users the world over: if a panel becomes damaged in action, all the soldiers have to do is unbolt it and replace it – a process that takes minutes.

By far the most significant difference between a saloon car and an off-roader however, is the latter's fitment of a transfer box to change between high and low ratio. In essence this results in two gearboxes: a high ratio one for on-road use and a low-geared one for off-roading. A set of low gears is vital for successful and safe off-roading, as you need the low speed and control that this gives for most types of terrain. Some off-roaders have lower ratios than others, although the majority of 4x4s fitted with a transfer box are

eminently capable. Vehicles that are notable for their lack of a transfer box include the Toyota RAV4, Land Rover Freelander and Daihatsu Terios, and none of these is suitable for serious use off-road. Instead these have been designed as on-roaders with a limited all-terrain capability.

Engine torque and power characteristics are also important for off-road vehicles. A high-revving engine that delivers its maximum torque in excess of 4,000 rpm is of little use off-road, as maximum pulling power should occur at low revs to prevent the driver having to constantly change gear while off the tarmac. For example, the Land Rover Tdi engine's maximum torque occurs at 1,800 rpm, which is ideal for all types of off-road applications. With the correct choice of ratio you should be able to crawl along in third

*Fig.14 The Land Rover Freelander is typical of the new wave of 4x4s entering the market. As it doesn't feature a transfer box its off-road potential is limited.*

*Fig.15 Off-road vehicles handle differently from saloons on the road, but with a little experience they can be made to perform.*

gear low for most off-road tracks, while a gentle application of throttle will provide instant torque to pull you through mud or up a steep hill.

One final point about off-roaders is a basic caution. Whereas saloons are designed to operate only on the road, 4x4 off-roaders are genuine all-terrain vehicles, and as such handle differently on the road from their lower and smaller counterparts. With experience a 4x4 can be made to take corners on-road at relatively high speeds, but there is less margin for error in a 4x4 than there is with a standard saloon. Although this book has not been written to discuss on-road driving techniques, it is worth being aware

that off-road vehicles will handle differently from saloons. As long as you don't try to attempt the impossible, you should encounter no problems.

## THE HISTORY OF 4x4

The majority of people believe that the great granddaddy of all four-wheel drive vehicles is the Willys Jeep, and to a certain extent they are right. However, the first vehicles to power all four wheels can be traced back much further than this. According to motoring historian James Taylor in his '4x4 Story' series in the magazine *Inter-*

*national Off-Roader*, the first 4x4 can be traced back as far as 1904. Built as a racer by the Amsterdam-based Spyker company, the vehicle used a separately mounted gearbox where two identical sets of gearwheels transmitted drive to the front and rear wheels. Although the Spyker had some success on the race circuit, it is believed that no more than four examples of this four-wheel drive oddity were produced as the transmission design was inherently unreliable.

It was the mechanization of the armed forces in the early years of the twentieth century that really pushed forward the development of the four-wheel drive system, and some primitive types of four-wheel drive truck are believed to have been used by both sides during the First World War. The US-built Marmon-Herrington four-wheel drive system was fitted to a variety of medium-capacity trucks during the 1930s and this was seen as an important step in gaining mainstream credibility for the advantages of four-wheel drive, with the company producing a large number for both military and civilian users. American commentators – with justification – have referred to the Marmon-Herrington as the 'granddaddy of the Jeep', as the company was responsible for downsizing four-wheel drive systems from the large military trucks of earlier decades.

It was not until 1940 however that four-wheel drive hit the mainstream, when the US military invited tenders for a smaller quarter-ton four-wheel drive vehicle that would eventually spawn the ubiquitous Jeep. Before the Second World War, the US military had realized that the horse was no longer a viable option for the modern battlefield, but it wasn't until the start of hostilities and the possibility of American involvement that work began on designing an appropriate vehicle.

Tenders were requested from 135 motor manufacturers, with an almost infeasibly tight deadline of 49 days before delivery of

*Fig.16 An early Jeep chassis showing the basic but rigid structure that was the key to its success. Most modern off-roaders maintain the same basic elements of a rigid chassis, torquey engine and selectable four-wheel drive.*

the first prototype. Not surprisingly then, only two manufacturers bothered to produce vehicles: the Bantam Company of Pennsylvania and Willys-Overland of Ohio. After exhaustive trials, an order was made for a modified version of the Willys prototype which would eventually be built by Ford, thanks to their increased production capacity and proven mass-production lines.

After the war, demobbed examples of the Jeep became available on the civilian market, where they were quickly snapped up by farmers and landowners for use around their estates. Maurice Wilks of the British Rover Company was one such gentleman farmer, and he quickly drew up plans for his own version of the Jeep using the basic chassis and transmission, but with a Rover saloon car engine up front. A different set of body panels was also designed to differentiate between this British product and the original Jeep, and the resulting vehicle was eventually launched at the Amsterdam motor show in 1948, where it became known as the Land Rover.

By now, the advantages of a light four-wheel drive vehicle for agricultural use were clear, and developing nations also became keen on using Land Rovers and Jeeps for day-to-day transport on their rough-and-ready roads. The Japanese became involved with their own versions of the light four-wheel drive, and a whole new breed of vehicle developed.

Back in America, manufacturers such as General Motors, Ford and International

*Fig.17 Range Rover number one pictured with its larger and more powerful heir. Launched in 1970, the Range Rover was the first 4x4 to combine saloon-car comfort and go-anywhere ability.*

*Fig.18 First-time off-roaders will notice some extra levers and switches in the cockpit of their 4x4 . . .*

were taking four-wheel drive vehicles to the next logical step: that of using the all-wheel drive capability for the leisure sector of the market. Up until then, four-wheel drives were very much designed for work – you used the all-terrain capability to get you some-where that you needed to go, rather than for a quick pleasure trip up into the hills. By combining the relative luxury of a saloon car with a rugged four-wheel drive system, customers could have a vehicle that they could use for work as well as for weekends away with the family.

These early American vehicles spawned what is without doubt the spiritual precursor of all modern 4x4s: the British-designed Range Rover launched in June 1970. No other vehicle until then had managed to combine the luxury of a car with the all-terrain capability of a 4x4 as seamlessly, and the vehicle became an overnight success at home and abroad. It is testament to the soundness of the original design that the

Range Rover would continue almost un-altered for another twenty-six years, before being replaced by its larger and more powerful heir.

By the mid-1970s, a number of Range Rover 'clones' were available (most notably from the Japanese), and by the end of the 1980s the new 'leisure' 4x4 was firmly established as the new growth area within the car market. The 1990s have seen a new breed of smaller all-wheel drive leisure vehicles that, although lacking a transfer box and with only limited ground clearance, should perform fairly competently off the tarmac.

Make no doubt about it, the four-wheel drive vehicle is here to stay. Whether designed for on-road posing in California, or for a hard-working life in the deserts of Africa, the basic principle remains: having an all-terrain capability is a passport to adventure – whether or not the driver ever makes that magic transition to four-wheel drive and heads for the hills.

## FOUR-WHEEL DRIVE EXPLAINED

As discussed above, four-wheel drive vehicles are somewhat more complex underneath than conventional two-wheel drive vehicles. Sitting in the driver's seat, first-time off-roaders will notice a variety of extra gear levers and switches, many of which are a complete mystery. It is vitally important that owners of off-road vehicles understand what these levers do, as their correct operation is imperative if you are to get the most from the four-wheel drive system that is fitted.

For example, it is a common misconception that all four-wheel drives are invincible off-road. People imagine that they can simply drive from the tarmac onto the mud and somehow the four-wheel drive system will automatically engage and they will keep going. Ask yourself how often you have seen an expensive four-wheel drive vehicle floundering in a wet grass field when it should be quite simple to drive across. If only that person had understood the simple principles of a four-wheel drive vehicle, they would probably have had no problem at all. Below we examine how four-wheel drive systems work in their most basic forms, before looking at them again in more detail in Chapter 4.

### Part-Time Four-Wheel Drive

Let us examine the part-time four-wheel drive system first, as this is by far the most common transmission set-up available on 4x4 vehicles. For normal road use, power is transmitted to the rear axle only, thus giving two-wheel drive or 4x2 configuration. For off-road use this is clearly of little advantage, so there is an extra lever (normally situated by the gear lever) to engage the front axle as well, creating four-wheel drive or 4x4.

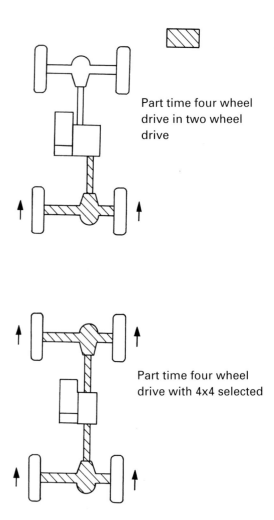

Part time four wheel drive in two wheel drive

Part time four wheel drive with 4x4 selected

*Fig.19 Diagram showing the part-time four-wheel drive system.*

There is a snag to this system, however, and that is to be found in the axle differentials that are fitted to all wheeled vehicles. Differentials are clever devices that all allow each wheel to turn at different speeds, enabling the vehicle to turn corners and release transmission wind-up on hard surfaces. For off-road use they have certain disadvantages, however, as when a wheel loses traction off-road the differential lets power escape via the easiest route, that is, the wheel that has the least traction. Unfortunately this means that the wheel that still has grip receives no power, and so the vehicle becomes stuck!

However, if we assume that the other axle still has traction and that the vehicle is in four-wheel drive, then the power being transmitted to this axle should be sufficient to pull the car out of trouble and hopefully to an area of better traction. In other words, all four-wheel drive means is that you can afford to lose traction to only one wheel – any more than this and you will become stuck.

You should never drive a part-time 4x4 system in four-wheel drive on the road as the front and rear wheels will tend to drive at different speeds as you corner. On a loose surface slight skidding will release the pressure, but on hard surfaces this cannot happen and the transmission will become 'wound up'. This can be identified by a stiffness when driving or by a difficulty in turning, and in severe cases this can only be released by jacking up a wheel and letting it turn freely.

## Full-Time Four-Wheel Drive

As their name suggests, full-time 4x4 systems constantly provide power to both axles in all conditions. To prevent the transmission from becoming wound up as discussed above, a third differential is fitted to the gearbox to allow each axle to rotate at its own speed as the vehicle travels around a corner on-road. This is because the front axle has to go further around a corner than the rear one, so the front axle has to be driven faster than the rear.

Once off-road, we encounter the same problem with axle differentials as the part-time system, although this time we have an additional problem to overcome – the

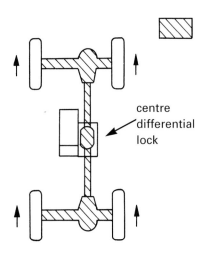

*Fig.20 Diagram showing the full-time four-wheel drive system.*

third differential in the gearbox. For example, if the gearbox differential is left open, a vehicle that is supposed to be permanent four-wheel drive can end up being one-wheel drive if power can find an easy route to exit via one wheel. To demonstrate this, all you need to do is put a set of rollers under one wheel and attempt to drive off with the centre differential open. Even with the best will in the world, you and the vehicle will go nowhere.

To overcome this, vehicles with permanent four-wheel drive feature a centre differential lock which effectively prevents the gearbox differential from working, creating a solid link that transmits power to both the front and rear axles, creating a set-up similar to the part-time system locked in four-wheel drive. In other words, power is shared between the front and rear axles so the worst-case scenario will be two wheels spinning in a cross-axle situation. In most cases however, having power transferred to both axles allows the other axle to push the vehicle through the obstacle.

Permanent four-wheel drive with manual centre differential lock is the system used in all Land Rover products since 1983, although Range Rovers from the 1990 model feature a Borg Warner transfer box with a viscous coupling which effectively operates the centre differential automatically whenever it is required.

## The Transfer Box

Off-roading is all about control, and you will soon find that a slow and gentle approach is the best way to tackle the majority of off-road obstacles. A low-ratio gearbox therefore is an absolute must for safe and controlled off-roading, and this set of low gears is normally accessed via a secondary set of reduction gears situated in the vehicle's transfer gearbox.

The transfer box has two sets of ratios: low and high, which basically speaking should be for off-road and on-road use respectively. The low ratio in most off-roaders features an extremely low first gear for descending steep hills, while third low will be approximately the same as first gear high. You should instinctively change to low ratio as you leave the tarmac, unless of course you require four-wheel drive for a snow-covered road or a gravel track where low ratio would be too slow for the reasonable ground conditions.

As well as using the low ratio gears off-road, having a crawler gear can be useful for other situations – for example, a hill start with a heavily loaded trailer, precision trailer reversing or any type of ultra-slow speed work where a crawl would be useful. We shall discuss the transfer box further in Chapter 4.

*Fig.21  The range of low gears accessed via the transfer box gives you perfect control for all off-road conditions.*

*Fig. 22 The latest Jeep Wrangler retains some styling cues from the original Jeep, but the four-wheel drive system is undoubtedly modern.*

## DIFFERENT TYPES OF 4x4

A quick leaf through the pages of any magazine dedicated to four-wheel drive vehicles will reveal just how many types of off-roader there are. From the most basic second hand Land Rover that costs a few hundred pounds through to a top-of-the-range Toyota Landcruiser or Range Rover priced in excess of £45,000, there is a 4x4 vehicle for everyone.

How do you choose which vehicle to buy and use, however? With so many manufacturers now offering 4x4s in their line up, there is more choice than ever before for the buyer of an off-road vehicle. Do you choose petrol or diesel? Manual or automatic? Basic off-roader or luxury version with an off-road capability? All these are questions that you should ask yourself before parting with your cash, and there will be some discussion later on in the book regarding the various merits/disadvantages of automatic versus manual and petrol versus diesel.

This section aims to look at three different types of off-roader available on the market, assessing each one's plus and minus points with regard to relatively serious off-roading and also day-to-day on-road use. It should be noted that there is no 'best vehicle' among each of these categories; instead we aim to show you how your intended use should influence your final choice of vehicle. Remember also that the vehicles we are discussing here are completely standard. The next chapter examines the various ways in which you can modify your vehicle to make it perform better off-road.

### Jeep Wrangler

Although a descendant of the original Willys MA, the modern Jeep Wrangler is just a little more luxurious and powerful than its 1940s counterpart. Using styling cues that can be traced back to the original wartime Jeeps, the vehicle looks remarkably similar to the

27

original model, right down to its classic grille and much talked about round headlamps. Nevertheless this is where the similarities end, as the modern Wrangler features a more luxurious interior, more sophisticated transmission system, driver and passenger airbags and an emission-controlled fuel-injected petrol engine.

Available in the UK in right-hand drive form since 1997, the Wrangler is what might be termed as a no-nonsense off-roader in the same mould as the Land Rover Defender which has an equally illustrious heritage. Looking at the vehicle, we can note the straight body panels, minimal front and rear overhangs and good ramp breakover angle – features that are handy for serious off-road use.

The vehicle is available with a 2.5 or 4.0 litre petrol engine mated to a five-speed manual or four-speed automatic transmission. The transfer box offers full or part-time four-wheel drive and there is a good set of low-ratio gears for extreme off-road use. Although the vehicle is perfectly civilized for trips on-road, this is by no means a top-of-the-range luxury machine. Instead the emphasis is very much on fun motoring, with a natural bias towards off-road use. Both engines deliver prodigious amounts of low-down torque to keep you moving off-road, although the straight six 4.0 litre version has an obvious advantage over the smaller 2.5 litre version.

Whereas previous generation Jeeps (including the previous Wrangler) featured leaf springs, the latest Wrangler features coil springs for superior axle articulation. Consequently the off-road ride is excellent, while suspension travel is more than adequate for most off-tarmac situations. Long suspension travel enables all four wheels to remain in contact with the ground over undulating terrain, and as we have discussed before, keeping the wheels on the ground means that you have more chance of maintaining traction.

In short, the 1997 Jeep Wrangler is an excellent choice for off-roading. Short overhangs and minimal bodywork mean that the vehicle is unlikely to sustain any panel damage even in the tightest of off-road sections, while the gearbox and transmission have been carefully designed with extreme off-roading in mind. The low ratio is deep enough to offer excellent engine-braking downhill, while driving in third gear low allows the vehicle to sit perfectly on the engine's torque curve, ready for smooth power delivery when it is required. A range of approved Jeep accessories are also available, allowing you to modify and improve your Wrangler still further for off-road use.

## Mitsubishi Shogun SWB

If one were playing devil's advocate, it could be said that the Mitsubishi Shogun is the next step up from the Jeep Wrangler in the 4x4 hierarchy. Whereas the Wrangler has been designed with extreme off-roading very much in mind, the Shogun manages to strike the difficult balance between being a competent off-roader and a comfortable on-roader.

From the outside, the Shogun looks rather more car-like, with more rounded body panels, 'proper' full-size plastic bumpers and a slightly less rugged profile. Inside it is the same story: the fascia wouldn't look out of place in a family saloon, while electric windows and other electronic gadgets pander to the needs of the modern motorist.

On-road, the Shogun is more comfortable on long journeys, with a choice of 2.5 litre turbocharged diesel or V6 petrol models mated to a manual or automatic transmission. The vehicle's top speed is also higher than the Wrangler's, and the interior with its fully trimmed carpets and comfortable seats puts it right up there with the average family saloon.

*Fig.23 The short-wheelbase Mitsubishi Shogun manages to strike the difficult balance of being a competent off-roader and a comfortable on-roader.*

Nevertheless the Shogun is a competent off-roader. The basic short-wheelbase model pictured here has short front and rear overhangs for excellent manoeuvrability in tight off-road situations, while the four-wheel drive system includes the fitment of a lockable rear differential in certain models to really keep things on the move.

In its most basic form, the Shogun is a superb compromise between off-road mud plugger and on-road family saloon. It has the comfort and inoffensive road manners to please those owners coming from cars, while its off-road performance goes way beyond the requirements demanded by most owners. The prudent addition of a winch and the fitment of some off-road tyres should make the short wheelbase Shogun pretty well unstoppable off-road.

## Range Rover 4.6 HSE

At the other end of the spectrum from the Wrangler, the top-of-the-range Range Rover 4.6 HSE looks more like an executive limousine than a serious mud plugger. Inside, leather and walnut abound, while electronically controlled seats, computer-controlled air conditioning and a plethora of electronic equipment help justify its hefty price tag.

From the interior at least it seems difficult to imagine that this sophisticated piece of engineering can ever be a capable off-roader – surely it is just too precious to ever take seriously off-road? However, for those owners brave enough to risk possible panel damage, the Range Rover 4.6 HSE is an extremely capable off-road machine.

With permanent four-wheel drive, a

*Fig.24 Although most owners wouldn't dream of taking their Range Rover 4.6 HSE seriously off-road, the vehicle is extremely capable.*

powerful and torquey engine and a number of unique features such as electronic air suspension and traction control, the Range Rover is an excellent off-road performer. But with a longer rear overhang than either of the vehicles featured above and a conspicuous front spoiler, extra care is necessary if expensive damage isn't to result. It just takes a little courage and some prudence to guide it through the mud.

Of all the electronic gadgets featured on the second generation Range Rover, the electronic air suspension is one area that deserves particular attention, as it effectively increases the vehicle's ride height, thus counteracting the Range Rover's reduced approach and departure angles. The system will also sense when a wheel has left the ground completely, and will attempt to compensate by dropping the offending wheel still lower to obtain grip.

If no traction is found, the Range Rover operates its electronic traction control system which uses the brakes and the ABS to bring a spinning wheel to a halt. By transferring the power from the path of least resistance in this way (see the explanation of 4x4 systems above), the ETC system should prevent excessive wheelspin, allowing the vehicle to continue onwards without becoming cross axled or stuck.

As well as being a competent player off-road, on-road the 4.6 HSE is exquisite, with above legal speeds all too easy to reach. Cocooned within the sumptuous interior, road noise and engine roar are almost non-existent, while the handling and general roadholding of the vehicle is also much improved. It seems as though the 4.6 HSE is one of the best on-tarmac performers in the 4x4 market today, although the story doesn't stop there. Providing that you are prepared for a few scratches and treat the vehicle with the respect it deserves, the Range Rover 4.6 HSE is a surprisingly competent off-road performer as well.

# 3 Equipping Your Vehicle – Accessories and 'Musts'

Although most showroom-standard off-road vehicles are extremely capable in their most basic form (see Chapter 2), it is advantageous to modify and equip your vehicle before venturing seriously off-road. Modifications may be restricted to a new set of off-road tyres that feature larger side lugs to cope better with muddy conditions or, for the really serious, a complete vehicle package including axle differential locks, off-road suspension and a winch to enable you to recover yourself should you become irretrievably stuck.

Even if you don't plan to modify your vehicle at all, there is a basic off-road kit that you need to invest in before venturing off the tarmac for the first time. These items are vital for your own personal safety, the safety of the vehicle and to ensure that you are sticking to a legal right of way. We'll discuss

*Fig.25 Modifying your vehicle can make it much more capable off-road.*

the ideal off-road kit in more detail in this chapter, but you should always ensure that you have this minimum of equipment wherever you go.

## THE BASIC KIT

Deciding what to take and what to leave behind when off-roading is a difficult choice. You have to balance the weight of the equipment with the loadspace available, and also consider how much of that equipment you are actually likely to need. Some hardened off-roaders believe that you can never have too much equipment, and they weigh their vehicles down with almost every conceivable gadget imaginable, most of which will never be used. As such we are not recommending

that you load your vehicle down to the gunwales with kit, but there is a core list of equipment that you should always take with you when off-roading. This comprises:

- A standard 4.5m (15ft) nylon tow-rope (*not* the type sold for on-road towing in most garages)
- An 8m (25ft) Kinetic Energy Recovery Rope (KERR)
- A shovel with a pointed blade.
- A tree strop.
- An assortment of bow and 'D' shackles.
- A basic tool kit
- A first-aid kit
- A vehicle-mounted fire extinguisher with easy access
- A large, durable bag in which to store this equipment.

*Fig.26 If you were to carry all the off-road equipment you might possibly need it would look like this. Naturally this causes storage problems of its own!*

This equipment will allow you to recover the vehicle should you become stuck, which – let's face it – is pretty likely. Even if you decide to leave everything else at home, you should never consider driving off-road without a sturdy medium-length rope and a couple of shackles. Getting stuck without the means to recover yourself will without doubt ruin your day.

Another useful piece of kit is the Kinetic Energy Recovery Rope or KERR. This is a 'sprung' rope that is designed to stretch and then contract under tension, thus increasing the effective pull through the use of stored kinetic energy. It is important to use this rope correctly to get the best from it, and you should also be aware of the possible dangers if the KERR is used incorrectly. We shall discuss the KERR and its safe use in Chapter 6.

It is hoped that you will never need to use

the tool kit, fire extinguisher and first-aid kit that should be installed in your off-roader, but for obvious reasons it is worth carrying all three items when venturing off-road. Nevertheless, it is important to know what to do with them should an emergency arise, so we recommend a basic mechanics' course and some first-aid training to really make full use of them.

Finally you should consider taking along a few spare parts for emergency use, just in case you damage or break something mechanical or electrical while out in the field. We recommend the following as a minimum requirement:

- Spare fan belt
- Spare distributor cap
- Spare fuel filter
- Spare bulb set
- Oil, brake/clutch fluid and water.

*Fig.27 Always carry a fire extinguisher, otherwise your vehicle may end up like this.*

*Fig.28 A hi-lift jack is an extremely useful tool to have off-road, although it isn't compatible with every 4x4.*

If you intend to tackle some really serious tracks, you might also like to consider taking spare halfshafts, a steering arm, track rod and some universal joints to cater for almost every eventuality. Although you will probably be able to get hold of these items relatively easily if you break down while off-roading in the UK, carrying such items with you is a must if you are taking your vehicle on expedition to foreign parts.

## 'NICE TO HAVES'

On top of the basic list of equipment discussed above, there are several 'nice to have' items with which you might like to consider equipping yourself as you become more adventurous. This chapter intends to introduce you to these items as a brief introduction, and we shall discuss their full use in Chapter 6 which covers recovery techniques.

## The Hi-Lift Jack

As mentioned earlier, the hi-lift jack is a useful tool to have when venturing off-road. As well as serving as a heavy-duty jack for changing a wheel while off-road, it can be put to a number of other uses, especially when recovering a stuck vehicle. Indeed, there are some situations when the use of a hi-lift can greatly expedite an otherwise very tricky recovery situation. For example when the author became stuck in a bog in Iceland, jacking the front of the vehicle out of the glutinous mud with the hi-lift jack broke the suction between the mud and the underside of the vehicle, thus allowing the winch to do its work and pull the vehicle free. Without the hi-lift, it is unlikely that the winch would have been powerful enough to pull the vehicle out unaided.

Nevertheless, despite the hi-lift's usefulness, it cannot be used on every 4x4 vehicle in its standard form. Unlike conventional

*Fig.29 Air bag jacks can be used for all sorts of off-road recovery situations . . .*

bottle or trolley-type jacks, the hi-lift cannot be positioned directly underneath the vehicle – instead, the protruding arm must be wedged under a flat, solid piece of the vehicle's bodywork or bumper. For more utilitarian off-roaders, such as the Land Rover or Jeep, this presents no problem as the jack can easily be placed underneath the front bumper or rear crossmember. For other 4x4s with plastic bumpers however, this is obviously an impossibility.

To overcome this, serious off-roaders fit special heavy-duty bumpers or side protection bars that can be used for jacking. Indeed, even the Land Rover Defender range needs special upgraded side sills if the user wants to hi-lift jack off the side of the vehicle. Nevertheless, despite the necessity for these bodywork modifications, never underestimate the usefulness of a hi-lift. The serious off-roader would never travel without one.

## The Exhaust Air Jack

As explained above, the hi-lift jack cannot be used with every 4x4 on the market thanks to its incompatibility with rounded body panels. However, a durable and long-reach jack is an extremely useful tool to have for serious off-road use, thus explaining the development of the inflatable air-bag jack which uses the vehicle's exhaust gases to extend itself.

The uses for the air jack off-road are similar in many ways to the hi-lift, so we shall not dwell on them unduly here. Suffice it to say that the airbag is in many ways more versatile than the hi-lift, thanks to its compatibility with virtually every 4x4 on the market. Nevertheless, the air jack does require some extra care to ensure correct and safe inflation and it is of little use should you be alone and stranded with a stalled engine.

If your vehicle is incompatible with a hi-lift jack, an air-bag jack should be high on your equipment wish list.

## The 'Tirfor' Hand Winch

Should you be unable to afford an electric or engine-driven winch for the front of your vehicle, then the tirfor hand winch is an excellent substitute. Weighing just a few kilos, this relatively simple mechanical gadget will allow you to recover yourself from the worst off-road situations providing you have plenty of time and muscle!

Operating via a ratchet mechanism, moving the tirfor's handle backwards and forwards slowly pulls a wire rope through the device's jaws and, providing the load being pulled doesn't exceed the tirfor's maximum load, the stricken vehicle will be recovered. Although a useful substitute for the electric winch, many winch-equipped off-roaders take along a tirfor as well to provide extra 'insurance' or to act as a portable recovery device for rear or side pulls.

The author remembers one particularly arduous off-road trip organized by the late Tim Webster in which a tirfor saved the day. After a long steep climb that took several hours, the expedition's three Land Rover Ninetys (all of which were fitted with electric winches) had to be hand winched through a boggy section after each of the winch motors burnt out one by one – a case where a good dose of muscle and simple mechanics proved invaluable against electrical technology.

## Sand/Bridging Ladders

Although sand ladders were originally developed by the military for use in the desert, aluminium sand ladders or PSP (Pressed Steel Planking) have a number of other uses for the off-roader who has no intention of going near sand. For example, all Camel Trophy vehicles up until 1997 were fitted with four aluminium sand ladders for use in mud, and during the 1996 event in Kalimantan, sand ladders were also employed to provide extra grip when

*Fig.30 Two tirfor hand winches with their assorted accessories.*

*Fig.31 Aluminium sand ladders have a number of uses off-road, although their bulk can cause storage problems.*

traversing narrow log bridges, with the teams strapping them firmly to the logs using ratchet straps and rope.

Just as sand ladders are useful for keeping a vehicle above the sandy surface in the desert (spreading the vehicle's weight over a larger surface area prevents the vehicle from sinking), the same principle can be used to good effect when faced with deep mud and boggy terrain. Using a number of ladders joined together, a temporary 'walkway' can be constructed over soft ground, which in theory should be enough to prevent the vehicle from sinking down into the mud. Care must be taken not to sink the ladders themselves though, as they can be awkward to retrieve!

In addition to the relatively lightweight aluminium sand ladders, heavier duty steel bridging ladders are available for the serious off-roader. As well as offering similar 'flotation' capabilities, the strong steel ladders can be used to bridge gaps, serve as a ramp or provide extra grip when things get really rough. Note that unsupported aluminium ladders should never be used to bridge gaps, as they will inevitably bend and even snap when the weight of a vehicle is placed upon them.

It should be remembered however, that steel bridging ladders are unavoidably heavy and bulky and can provide storage problems. Whereas the aluminium versions are lighter, they are also relatively tricky to store thanks to their large bulk.

## Ground Anchors

When getting your vehicle unstuck using a winch you inevitably need an anchor to winch off. In most cases a stout tree is all you need (remembering to take care not to damage it) – but what if there are no trees

*Fig.32 When you can't find a tree or another vehicle to winch off a ground anchor will save the day.*

available and there are no other vehicles to assist? In this case you'll need a ground anchor, as it serves as a sturdy yet portable item to winch off. If you intend to do a lot of off-roading using just one vehicle (we don't recommend this for safety reasons), then you should definitely invest in a sturdy ground anchor so that you are able to effect a self-recovery in all situations should you become stuck.

Ground anchors come in all shapes and sizes, and each one has its plus and minus points. Generally speaking, Goodwinch T stakes or ORCA ground anchors seem to offer the best performance in general muddy conditions, although the somewhat unusual looking American-designed Pull Pal performs particularly well in sand or bog.

If you become stuck and do not have a ground anchor, digging a deep hole and placing the spare tyre inside at an oblique angle can provide an effective temporary ground anchor (see diagram), although this method does require rather a lot of effort and should only be used as a last resort.

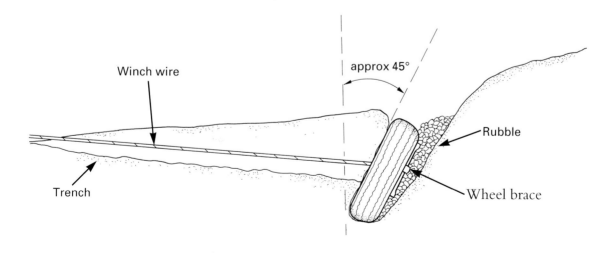

*Fig. 33 Burying a spare wheel for use as a ground anchor.*

# WHERE TO PUT THIS EQUIPMENT

The first rule when carrying equipment off-road is to make sure that it is stowed properly. As well as organizing the equipment so that it is easily accessible in a recovery situation (that is, have items that you will use regularly – such as ropes and shackles – easily to hand), having it well stored will prevent it from flying everywhere as the vehicle lurches and bounces its way across rough terrain.

Knowing how much equipment you have and whether or not your vehicle is used solely for off-roading will dictate how you decide to store your off-road recovery gear. If your 4x4 also serves as your day-to-day transport, you will probably want to store the majority of your recovery equipment in a large soft bag that can be kept in the luggage compartment.

Doing so will keep your carpets clean and allow you to remove it easily once a weekend's off-road fun has finished. If you are fortunate enough to have a vehicle solely for off-road use, then the large 'Action Packer' type of heavy-duty plastic boxes are ideal for storing large amounts of heavy off-road gear.

Either way, make sure that the bag or box is well strapped down in the rear loadbay, ideally using a heavy-duty nylon net secured to the vehicle's floor. Not only will this keep things secure while your vehicle is bouncing about off-road, but in the unlikely – but possible – event of a rollover, heavy items (such as shackles or a snatch block) will be kept secure rather than flying around in the passenger compartment. Don't ever rely on bungy straps to keep your gear in place as these will in time stretch and give way.

*Fig.34 Make sure that you can store all your off-road equipment safely.*

*Fig.35 A set of knobbly off-road 'mud terrain' tyres will significantly increase the capabilities of your 4x4.*

## OFF-ROAD TYRES

If there is one thing that will improve the off-road performance of a standard vehicle more than anything else it is a set of aggressively patterned off-road tyres. As the majority of 4x4 vehicles spend most of their time on the road, off-road vehicle manufacturers have – very wisely – biased their choice of tyres for tarmac use. As such, showroom standard off-roaders will have tyres that handle and perform excellently on the road but leave a lot to be desired in extreme off-road situations – most particularly in mud. Put two identical 4x4s next to each other in the same muddy conditions, and the one fitted with off-road tyres will get further without becoming stuck every time.

As with all aspects of off-roading, there is an inherent compromise when considering the off- and on-road capability of tyres. Aggressive off-road tyres will not handle as well on the tarmac, and you will find that road noise will increase and the ride will become more harsh. Remember also that aggressive off-road tyres will often be 'interesting' to drive on in the wet, being prone to skids under extreme braking and cornering.

Bearing this in mind, most off-road tyre manufacturers have developed an all-round 'compromise' tyre that has been designed to perform adequately in both on- and off-road situations. Although not the most high-performance tyre off-road, unless you intend to attempt something really extreme the 'all-terrain' type of tyre offers perhaps the most useful and cost-effective way of getting the most from your vehicle.

For the keener off-roader, it may be worth investing in a secondary set of wheels fitted with a set of aggressively patterned off-road tyres. This way you have the best type of tyre for both on- and off-road conditions, although it can be a hassle having to change them each time you want to go off-road. As with everything, you pay your money and take your choice!

Basically speaking, a good off-road tyre will feature a relatively aggressive tread pattern that will allow the tyre to 'bite' into soft ground, thus giving good grip and therefore traction. A well designed 'mud terrain' tyre will allow mud to fly out of its lugs easily with a little fast rotation, thus creating a useful self-cleaning effect that will prevent the tyre from clogging up and becoming like a slick. The tyre's lugs should also be slightly angled to give a certain amount of sideways resistance, thus stopping any possibility of a sideways slide with the vehicle positioned on a side slope.

41

*Fig.36 Compare the difference between this off-road tyre . . .*

*Fig.37 . . . and this on-road version.*

42

For rocky and desert conditions an aggressive tyre pattern is only of certain use – instead a strong and multiple-ply sidewall is particularly important. We have seen seemingly innocuous-looking rocks puncture a tyre through its sidewall, thus writing off the tyre and causing inconvenience all round. On the other side of the coin, we have also seen a damaged tyre with a significant nick taken out of its side wall do several thousand road miles, thanks to its strong multiple-ply structure. Nevertheless, driving on any type of damaged tyre is extremely dangerous and also illegal. Unlike our friend in the example above, never drive on damaged tyres unless in an absolute emergency.

As if the choice of tread pattern wasn't enough, tyre size is also an important factor when choosing the ideal off-road tyre. To a certain extent tyre size is limited by your vehicle's wheelarch dimensions, and unless you want to risk damaging both your vehicle's suspension components and bodywork you should never try to fit a tyre that is larger than the manufacturer's recommended limit. Of course, oversize tyres can be fitted if you are willing to make suspension modifications or cut away the bodywork, but you should seriously consider the possible effects on the vehicle's resale value before you start hacking away at the bodywork with an angle grinder!

Larger tyres have several benefits for off-road use, such as extra ground clearance with taller tyres and increased flotation with wider ones. Having more ground clearance is particularly useful while off-road, as you will be able to follow relatively deep ruts with little fear of becoming high centred. However, once again you are limited by the maximum size of tyres that can be fitted to

*Fig.38 Fitting tall tyres will allow your vechicle to traverse deep ruts with little fear of becoming stuck.*

your vehicle. On an off-road trip to Wales the author spent much time high centred in ruts thanks to his Range Rover's relatively 'low' 235/75 R16 tyres, while Land Rover Ninetys on the same trip fitted with larger diameter 7.50x16 tyres drove along the same tracks without becoming stuck. Remember that if you intend to buy a new set of off-road tyres it is worth buying the largest ones that will fit your vehicle.

Wider tyres than standard (such as 265/75 R16s) will offer greater flotation when traversing boggy areas as they offer a larger footprint to equivalent diameter narrow tyres. However, this effect can be disadvantageous, especially when the tyre will not bite down through loose mud to more grippy rock underneath. Generally speaking, oversized wide tyres are only useful for sand and rock, and you should consider your off-roading carefully before ordering a set.

Note also that in the UK it is a legal requirement not to have your tyres protruding outside the line of the vehicle's bodywork. Although you can fit flared wheelarches to overcome this, there is a limit to how far you can go!

## PROTECTION, ROLL CAGES AND SNORKEL

As you use your vehicle more and more off-road you will notice that things start to become bent underneath; particularly if you tend to favour more challenging tracks. All off-road vehicles have been designed to resist underside damage, with major components such as the exhaust system, gearbox and fuel tank having been tucked up out of harm's way between the chassis rails to avoid most scrapes and bashes. Nevertheless, axles,

*Fig.39 If you want to tackle rocky terrain like this, a set of steering guards is a worthwhile investment.*

*Fig.40 A roll cage will offer protection for you and your vehicle should you roll over. Everyone hopes that a roll cage will be the biggest waste of money ever!*

differentials and steering components are still vulnerable to the odd knock or scrape from rocks, tree roots or even compacted mud.

To overcome unnecessary damage, a number of firms manufacture solid bash plates for all types of 4x4 to protect the differentials, steering components and fuel tank from damage. Most of these simply bolt on to the chassis, providing a worthwhile investment against possible inconvenience and expensive damage.

By the same token, everyone who fits a roll cage to their off-roader hopes that it will be the biggest waste of money that they have ever spent. Nevertheless, for anyone intending to do some serious off-roading fitting a roll cage gives added peace of mind should the unthinkable happen. Not only will a roll cage protect your vehicle from serious damage in most cases, it will also protect you and your passengers.

Roll cages can be bought 'off the shelf' from companies such as Safety Devices, or they can be custom built to your own specifications by a specialist such as Drew Bowler. They can be fitted either internally or externally, although to offer maximum protection they must be welded either to the chassis or a major structural point of the vehicle. The author has seen one external roll cage that was bolted to the front decker panel of a Range Rover, and as such this would offer little protection should a roll-over occur. Check also that the quality of the welding is up to scratch, as this is another area that can be problematic with some unscrupulous manufacturers.

Another safety device that offers extra peace of mind when off-roading is the snorkel or high-level air intake. Although most 4x4 manufacturers do not recommend driving their vehicles in water higher than a thumb's length below the top of the wheels, most off-roaders (especially diesels) can be driven in relatively deep water with a little extra modification.

Of these the high-level air intake is the most important, as this allows the engine to breathe while being driven through deep water. Providing that the vehicle has been properly prepared and that there are no leaks in the system, most diesel engines can be totally submerged and still keep on running! We recommend buying a snorkel from a reputable company such as Mantec Services and having it installed professionally before attempting any serious wading with your pride and joy.

*Fig.41 If you want to tackle water this deep, a snorkel and axle breathers are imperative. Believe it or not, the engine kept running throughout this driver's submarine antics.*

*Fig.42 Locking axle differentials will enable you to maintain traction in extreme off-road situations like this.*

## LOCKING AXLE DIFFERENTIALS

Although some off-road vehicles feature locking axle differentials as standard (the Toyota Landcruiser for example) or limited slip differentials (Nissan Terrano/Isuzu Trooper, and so on), most manufacturers only offer locking axle differentials as an option.

The locking axle differential is not to be confused with the centre-locking differential that operates on the gearbox. Locking the differential on the axle provides a solid link between the two wheels on an axle, thus preventing any free spin associated with loss of traction (see Chapter 2). As such, they are very useful in cross-axle situations, or when a loss of traction on one side of the vehicle will result in your becoming stuck.

Several types of locking axle differential are available, but by far the most popular seems to be the Australian-made ARB Air Locker available for almost every type of off-road vehicle. Using compressed air to engage and disengage the specially made differential that replaces the standard unit, the air locker is instantly switched on and off using a dashboard-mounted switch. Unlike part-time 'automatic' differential locks (such as a limited slip differential) the driver selects the appropriate moment to switch the ARB Air Locker on, so it is important to only engage it when it is safe to do so .

There are some disadvantages however. Axle differential locks are generally very expensive to buy and install; they can cause axle components to break if not used properly, and it is almost impossible (and potentially damaging) to steer with the front axle differential locked. Nevertheless, if used with care and experience, the axle differential lock can make an off-road vehicle almost unstoppable. Note though that an axle locker is of little use if there is no traction available, say in extremely muddy conditions

*Fig.43 Specialist off-road suspension is a worthwhile investment for the serious off-roader.*

– instead you just have four wheels spinning uselessly instead of two!

## SUSPENSION MODIFICATIONS

As with standard fitment tyres, most off-road vehicles' suspension is a compromise when it leaves the factory. When off-road, your vehicle needs to be able to crawl over the terrain, so long travel and flexible suspension is a must.

There is a large variety of different suspension packages available for most types of off-roader, and it is beyond the scope of this book to go into each one individually. Suffice it to say that suspension kits designed specifically for off-road use are by far the most desirable, and these can be separated into two different types: those that maintain the standard ride height, and others that offer sometimes quite substantial amounts of lift to facilitate the fitment of larger wheels and tyres.

Either way, dampers designed for off-road use are generally heavier duty than the standard versions, although there is obviously a price premium to pay. The ideal dampers for off-roading are soft on compression but stiff on the rebound, while gas-filled dampers tend to be better suited to the intense movement associated with fast driving over rough terrain. Off-roaders built for fast desert

racing can feature up to six dampers per axle to share the load, and it stands to reason that the more dampers you have, the more reliable they will be in extreme conditions.

Fitting softer, more flexible suspension bushes is also highly recommended. Whereas standard bushes are normally made from rubber, a set formed from polyurethane will be harder wearing and therefore last longer than a standard set. When replacing the bushes however, make sure that the largest bushes pass the 'squeeze between two fingers' test. If you cannot squeeze the bush easily between your thumb and middle finger then it is too hard for off-road use and you shouldn't fit it.

*Fig.44 A winch is invaluable for extreme conditions.*

# WINCHES

A winch fitted to your vehicle provides a useful 'lifeline' for those inevitable times when you get stuck, although it use for 'recreational' off-roading is a fairly recent phenomenon. Winches have been fitted to off-road vehicles for many years, although they were primarily to be seen on working vehicles, such as those used by the electricity supply companies, British Telecom and HM Coastguard. These users needed them not only for self-recovery when the going got tough, but also for pulling cables up pylons and rescuing hapless individuals from the sides of cliffs.

Nevertheless, the usefulness and practicality of a winch soon became obvious to the growing band of hard-core off-roaders, while the increase in availability of electric winches from the mid-1980s meant that fitting kits for all types of 4x4 started to become available. Nowadays, the fitment of winches to off-road vehicles is becoming increasingly common, and given their usefulness for all types of recovery situations this is hardly surprising.

## Mechanical and Hydraulic Winches

Mechanical and hydraulic winches provide heavy-duty pulling power, as they make use of the vehicle's engine to operate. Mechanical versions run off the vehicle's power take off (PTO) with power taken directly from the engine, while hydraulic winches require the fitment of a hydraulic pump to operate, which once again is connected to the gearbox PTO.

The main benefit of mechanical and hydraulic winches is their unfaltering pulling power. As neither make use of an electric motor, there is no drain upon the battery or vehicle electrical system. In the case of mechanical winches, the speed and

strength of pull can be governed by the gear selected and the amount of throttle applied, while hydraulic winches give a consistently smooth pull thanks to the powerful hydraulic system that is required to operate them. Watching either type of these winches operate is very impressive, as they seldom seem phased by the severity of the pull.

There are disadvantages to both types however. Firstly, if the engine has died and cannot be restarted, both types of winch are completely useless – something that can be problematic, especially if the vehicle being recovered has died in water! Secondly, the requirement of a PTO limits the type of vehicle that these winches can be fitted to. Few modern 4x4s have the provision for a PTO, with the notable exception of the Land Rover Defender range.

As such, only the select few can have these types of winches fitted to their vehicles, and their high purchase price might also affect their selection. Although mechanical and hydraulic winches offer the ultimate in pulling power, they are a relative rarity in the recreational field of off-roading.

## Electric Winches

As described above, the fitment of electric winches to off-road vehicles used for recreational purposes is a fairly recent phenomenon – indeed, the majority of electric winches sold to off-roaders today were originally designed for use by recovery trucks when pulling broken-down vehicles onto the back of flatbed lorries.

The classic off-road recovery winch is the Warn 8274, which although still available today was originally launched in 1974. The 8274 offers a strong, fast pull and is a popular choice among the off-road fraternity. However, the Warn is rather cumbersome and can often not be fitted directly to the chassis, requiring the additional expense of a specially manufactured winch bumper.

This need for 'discreet' mounting resulted in the development of the low-profile electric winch, of which there are a large number. The most popular are made by Superwinch or Warn, and both manufacturers produce a variety of different power ratings for different sized vehicles. For standard-sized off-roaders (anything from a Land Rover Defender 90 to a Range Rover) the Superwinch X9 offers 8,500lb of pull, while the Warn X9000i gives 9,000lb. Smaller vehicles (such as the Suzuki Vitara or Daihatsu Sportrak) will be able to fit winches with lower power ratings, while if you own anything larger than a Toyota Landcruiser, a much heavier duty winch is advised.

### Equipment for Winches

Once you have fitted a winch to your vehicle, you will need to buy some additional equipment to make full use of its potential. These range from 'must haves' to 'nice to haves', all of which vary according to the severity of the terrain you intend to tackle. Most winch manufacturers and suppliers produce a winch kit bag which contains the key items that you need, and we shall examine these and their various uses in Chapter 6.

## EXPEDITION MODIFICATIONS

In addition to the equipment and accessories listed above, if you intend taking your off-roader on an overland expedition there are a number of specific and useful modifications and accessories that are vital for a safe and trouble-free journey. These range from specific recovery equipment to general items (such as a strong tent) that will make your adventure of a lifetime more comfortable.

The purpose of an expedition vehicle, put

*Fig.45 The Series III Land Rover Safari has long been an expedition favourite.*

simply, is to transport two or more people from A to B with relative comfort, safety and reliability, allowing for the possibility that point A and point B may be separated by several thousand miles of dirt, mud and unmade roads, accompanied perhaps by extreme weather conditions. The long-wheelbase Land Rover has for some time been the expeditioners' favourite, with the older Series III 109 Safari remaining ever popular.

The Series III's basic construction and mechanics means that there is very little to go wrong, and if anything does it should be relatively straightforward to mend. However, if a Series III Land Rover is your preferred choice of vehicle, you should be prepared to spend a decent amount of money on fully refurbishing it before leaving. Maybe it would be better to buy a newer vehicle, although anything with complex electronics or with poor 'on the ground' spares coverage should be avoided.

Critical to the selection, design and preparation of an expedition vehicle is the knowledge of where you are going. If you intend to explore an area with large amounts of sand or mud, excessive vehicle weight will be a problem, while a vehicle that is too large or heavy will limit where you can explore safely. Conversely a vehicle that is too small will leave you frustrated, tired and travel-weary after only a few days on the road – remember that on a long expedition, the vehicle is your mobile home for the duration. It will serve as somewhere to sleep and eat, as well as being your sole means of getting from A to B. When choosing an expedition vehicle bear this simple question in mind: how far off the beaten track can you get and still be comfortable when you turn off the engine?

This question of comfort is perhaps one of the key points in the selection and modification of an expedition vehicle. Will your trip take you several months or just a few weeks? If the former, you should consider very seriously some sort of 4x4 camper, or at least a vehicle modification that allows you to sleep inside (or on top of!) your vehicle. The climatic conditions are also very important to consider. If it's going to be extremely hot on a day-to-day basis (temperatures in excess of 30°C) then you might like to think about a vehicle with air conditioning, while a well insulated vehicle with a good heater is important for expeditions heading for sub-zero temperatures. Bear in mind however that air conditioning is something else to go wrong, so you should only have it if you really consider that it would be otherwise impossible to cope with the heat.

Your own safety and that of your vehicle is also important. The ability to cook your own

*Fig.46 Preparing your vehicle for your own requirements is extremely important when embarking on a long-range off-road expedition.*

food and filter your water is important if you are heading for an area where food and water hygiene is poor when compared to Western standards. A simple gas cooker or Trangia is useful for cooking, while a catodyne limestone water pump will let you drink river water with a little prudence. Protection from the elements is also important, as are mosquito nets for fitment over the windows when travelling in an area where disease-transmitting insects are rife. Sturdy vehicle locks and even mesh screens for the windows may also be advisable if you intend leaving your vehicle unattended for more than a couple of hours. For really remote regions, a satellite telephone offers constant emergency communications, and although it is expensive to buy and use, the satphone could well be a life saver.

As for specific equipment for off-road expeditions, a front-mounted winch is an important addition for self-recovery purposes if you intend to travel solo. A good set of off-road tyres with at least two spares is also imperative, while the ever-useful hi-lift jack should also be high on the equipment list. If you intend travelling in sandy areas, a set of four aluminium sand ladders will be of enormous benefit, while a snorkel with a cyclonic pre-cleaner should be fitted for wet or excessively muddy conditions. Finally some sort of underside protection would be advisable for the vulnerable steering components.

Luxuries would include an ARB Air

Locker, a roll cage and any additional underside protection. Before bolting on any extra bits and pieces it is worth remembering the weight penalties synonymous with large amounts of kit. At all times keep equipment and accessories to a minimum – that way you will avoid placing unnecessary stress on the vehicle and its components.

## Roof Racks

The roof rack is a useful addition to have on any off-roader being used on expedition, but you should be aware that there are just as many disadvantages as there are advantages. Although the roof rack provides useful extra storage space outside the vehicle, the temptation to overload it is a dangerous

*Fig.47 A sturdy roof-rack provides useful extra storage for long-range expeditions, although you should be careful not to overload them.*

possibility. A roof rack that is carrying more weight than it is designed for will place stress upon the vehicle, while a top-heavy vehicle will be more susceptible to tipping over thanks to its higher centre of gravity.

When packing a vehicle for expedition you should ideally store all heavy objects as low down in the vehicle as possible, which means that items such as spare wheels and full jerry cans should be located within the vehicle. Lighter items such as bags full of clothes are perfect for storage on the roof rack, although you should bear in mind that these might be an attractive proposition for the opportunistic thief. Whatever you place on the roof-rack, make sure that it is securely tied down and covered by a thick tarpaulin to protect it from the elements.

There are several different types of roof rack, although only the heaviest duty type (made from galvanized steel) is appropriate for expedition use. The lighter type should only be used for on-road use or for transporting small bags and skis. An alternative to the roof rack is the ABS plastic Thule roof box that is designed to carry bags and light goods only.

Another useful accessory that can be used with the full-length roof-rack is the roof tent. While on expedition in the wild, sleeping on the ground can be dangerous thanks to hordes of wild animals or creepy-crawlies. The roof tent gets you off the ground and as an additional benefit, it is quick to erect as well as folding well out of the way when not in use.

## Long-Range Fuel and Water Tanks

For long journeys far away from civilization an extra long-range fuel tank is an excellent idea, as it allows you to carry an extra quantity of fuel within the vehicle, rather than having to rely on external or roof-rack-mounted jerry cans. Available from twelve to

300 litres in capacity, the tanks can be custom made or they can be bought 'off the shelf' from specialist expedition suppliers.

Specially made water tanks are also a worthwhile addition, again to help keep items of heavy weight as low down within the vehicle as possible. Nevertheless, it is important that extra fuel and water tanks are clearly marked, as the consequences of filling a tank with the wrong liquid doesn't bear thinking about!

## Global Positioning System (GPS)

The Global Positioning System or GPS is an extremely sophisticated electronic device that has been in use by mariners for years, but has only recently become commonplace amongst off-roaders. Using a network of twenty-four satellites orbiting the earth, the GPS unit receives distance and time signals, and by using triangulation it calculates its position on earth. With four satellites locked into the GPS, the unit can achieve three-dimensional accuracy, which means that it can display altitude in addition to latitude and longitude.

As the GPS was originally developed by the US military to aid its soldiers in battle, the worldwide system has been programmed with certain errors to prevent foreign powers employing the system to the same advantage as the US government. As such, you can never be entirely sure of the GPS unit's accuracy, although the latitude and longitude displayed should be within 25 metres of your actual position. For off-road use this is more than sufficient.

But what can GPS offer the off-roader? Although a luxury item while off-roading in Europe, the GPS is an almost indispensable piece of kit when driving across the desert or any barren area where there are no obvious tracks. Assuming that you have a map that shows the coordinates of the point you want

*Fig.48 The remarkable Global Positioning System (GPS) uses satellite technology to pinpoint your position anywhere in the world.*

to go to, simply enter these coordinates into the GPS unit and after a little calculation, the unit will point out the correct direction of travel, assuming that you can go in a straight line. If not, the GPS will constantly point out the right direction until you can get back on track. In the desert where there is a distinct lack of landmarks and decent mapping, this feature is invaluable unless, of course, you are capable of precise solar navigation!

Another useful feature that is available on most GPS units is the ability to plot your route by the regular insertion of your position. Should you take a wrong turn and want to retrace your steps, simply head for the last coordinates entered into the unit (known as a waypoint), and this should take you back whence you came.

Despite the usefulness of the GPS in desert conditions, there are benefits to using a GPS in the UK. For example, the ability to pinpoint your exact location is of use when driving tracks that are marked on the map, but are indistinguishable on the ground. Likewise, should you be lost on a mountain in fog or cloud, simply look at the GPS's co-ordinates and you will instantly be able to find your position on the relevant map.

Most GPS units are extremely portable, as they are designed to be handheld by walkers. As a result, storing them in an off-roader is easy. The only prerequisite is that the antenna has a clear view of the sky so that it can obtain a clear fix on the satellites. Placing the GPS on the dashboard is one solution, although this can often result in a loss of service when the angle of the satellites being tracked falls underneath the solid roof. By far the best solution is to fit an external vehicle-mounted antenna that allows you to plumb in the GPS unit every time you go off-roading. Most fitting kits allow the GPS to be removed when not in use, thus removing any possible temptation for the thief.

# MODIFYING YOUR VEHICLE

Before going any further, it should be made clear that you don't need all of the above to go off-roading. However as we explained earlier, the more that you modify your vehicle, the more capable it will be off-road. Off-road preparation is expensive though, so you should really draw up a list of priorities before going off to your nearest equipment supplier and offering up your plastic.

As we discussed, there is a basic list of equipment that you simply must have before venturing off-road, but everything else is optional. It just depends on your budget and the type of off-roading you want to do. If all you want is a vehicle in which to explore a few easy green lanes, then a showroom-standard 4x4 fitted with off-road tyres is probably all you need – but, if you intend taking your vehicle on a three-month expedition across Africa, then you will need to look very seriously at the sort of modifications that will make your journey easier and safer.

Below, we look at two different types of off-road vehicle – the Camel Trophy Discovery and Jeep Cherokee Rubicon – both of which have been seriously modified to cope with the demands their drivers will be putting on them off-road. It should be said that both vehicles are probably the ultimate as far as off-road preparation goes, and you may like to examine the various modifications and equipment carried, tailoring their ideas to your own needs and wants.

## Case Study 1 – Camel Trophy Discovery

Few people interested in off-roading can be unaware of the Camel Trophy. Probably the biggest four-wheel drive adventure on earth, every year the Camel challenges twenty teams from around the world to drive in some of the most inhospitable regions of the world. From seemingly impenetrable jungle tracks to the barren wastes of the desert, the competitors on the Camel Trophy have been to the ends of the earth – and back – using much-modified Land Rover vehicles.

Since its launch in 1989, the Land Rover Discovery has been the vehicle chosen by Camel to take the thousands of punishing off-road miles in its stride. However, although the vehicles used on the event are showroom standard in terms of bodywork, engine and transmission, the rest of the vehicle has been substantially modified to cope with the harsh off-road conditions demanded by the event. All these modifications have been designed to make the vehicle more capable and durable, and few that have taken part in a Camel Trophy can have much doubt as to their effectiveness.

The Discovery was first used on the Camel Trophy in 1990, where the teams explored areas of eastern Siberia in the first international motoring event held in the former Soviet Union. Development work to modify the vehicle was carried out by Land Rover's Special Vehicles department even before the Discovery was officially launched in late 1989. Using experience gained from nine years of Camel Trophy, each modification was made with a specific purpose in mind, and many ideas could equally be applied to your own vehicle. Likewise, ex-Camel Trophy vehicles make an ideal basis for an expedition vehicle – although some repair and restoration work may have to be carried out on well-used vehicles!

Taking the four-door TDi-engined

*Fig.49 The Camel Trophy Discovery is an excellent example of a vehicle modified for specific off-road use.*

*Fig.50 Another view of the Camel Trophy Discovery.*

Discovery as a base, Land Rover Special Vehicles have designed a vehicle that is without doubt the ultimate off-road Discovery. Note that the turbo diesel engine was chosen in preference to the V8, thanks to the diesel engine's impressive wading ability, its low fuel consumption and the generally easy availability of diesel fuel in the more remote areas of the world. These are three factors that help make a diesel engined off-roader the ideal choice for any long-range expedition.

Basically, the modifications that Special Vehicles have made to the Discovery can be divided into three main categories: safety, protection and performance enhancing. Additions such as a full internal roll-cage, heavier duty suspension and rear dog guard can be classed in the safety category; underside bash plates and the bush guard wire offer protection for exposed components; while the purposeful off-road tyres, 8,500lb winch and high-level air intake no doubt help hone the Discovery's already excellent off-road ability. Custom-made waterproof cases, along with a large quantity of off-road equipment help complete the very tidy package of modifications, leaving the observer in no doubt that this is a vehicle designed to perform.

Below, we list the modifications and equipment carried in full. As you can see, the vehicles and their equipment have certainly been well thought-out!

*Suspension:*
This has been upgraded to cope with the vehicle's additional weight, which – apart from the extra accessories – includes four adults and all their clothes and food for three weeks on the event.

Front: heavy-duty single rate coil springs with standard hydraulic dampers.

Rear: heavy-duty triple rate coil springs with additional centre-mounted helper springs. Single hydraulic dampers.

*Wheels and Tyres:*
On events pre-1997, the Camel Trophy Discoverys featured 16in Land Rover Defender-type steel disc wheels fitted with 700 x 16 Michelin XZL radial off-road tyres. However, in 1997 these were changed to 16in alloy wheels fitted with BF Goodrich Mud-Terrain tyres to suit the changing nature of the event.

*Additional Features, External:*
- Matt black bonnet – to prevent reflection from the roof-mounted spotlights.
- Two bonnet retaining clips – used to facilitate quick entry to the engine bay. They also keep the bonnet securely in place during some of the more arduous sections!
- Bull bar incorporating two driving lamps and the winch remote control socket.
- Superwinch Husky 8,500lb electric winch.
- Front-mounted galvanized steel steering guard manufactured by Safety Devices.
- Two 3.5ton towing hitches mounted directly to the chassis.
- Fully sealed raised air intake manufactured by Mantec Services – includes remote axle and gearbox breathers. Providing the seals are in good order it should be possible to drive the vehicle in water up to windscreen level with this modification, and many drivers have!
- Bush guard wire running from the bull bar to the roof rack. This prevents rogue branches from coming into contact with the windscreen, and also provides a clearer view for the driver when driving through dense foliage.
- Rear door-mounted ladder to roof rack.
- Rear-mounted spot lamp.
- Rear lamp guards.
- 5ton towing hitch on the rear bumper.
- Heavy duty galvanized steel fuel tank guard.
- Full length roof rack that is mounted directly through the roof onto the internal

roll cage.
- Two front-mounted spot lamps recessed flush to the front of the roof rack.
- Two front-mounted flood lamps recessed flush to the front of the roof rack.

*Additional Features, Internal:*
- Full internal roll cage manufactured by Safety Devices. This has been specifically designed for the Discovery and has been well incorporated into the interior. On Camel Trophy Kalimantan '96, seven Discoverys sustained roll-overs. Thanks to the roll cage, no-one was seriously injured and all the vehicles went on to complete the event.
- Terratrip electronic trip meter – used for highly accurate distance readings, and for rally-style distance/time calculations.
- Satellite navigation equipment (GPS).
- Vehicle compass.
- Waterproof seat covers and rubber floor mats.
- Flexible map lamp mounted on the transmission tunnel.
- VHF radio and satellite telephone.
- Two fire extinguishers.
- First-aid kit.
- Rear compartment dog guard. Installed to prevent any heavy items stored in the loadbay penetrating the interior cabin space in the event of a roll-over.
- Two waterproof aluminium food boxes designed to fit underneath a wooden 'parcel shelf'.
- Two x 22l fuel cans (stored either side of the wooden shelf).
- Two x 22l water cans.
- One spare parts box.
- One tool kit.
- Solid metal tow bar.
- Voltage indicator.
- Internal winch control socket.

*Additional Equipment Carried:*
- Four fully waterproof 'Pelican' cases.
- Two spare wheels – one on the rear door, the other mounted on the roof rack.
- A felling axe (carried on the roof rack in a special holder).
- A pointed shovel (carried on the roof rack in a special holder).
- A pick axe (carried on the roof rack in a special holder).
- Four aluminium sand ladders (bolted either side of the roof rack using wing nuts).
- An assortment of tow ropes, all with hooks at either end.
- Heavy-duty winch control.
- Hand spotlamp with 12v connector – the female socket is incorporated into the dashboard.
- Winch bag, including gloves, shackles, tree strop and pulley block.
- An airbag exhaust jack.
- A volcano kettle.
- A catodyne water purifier and pump.

## Case Study 2 – Jeep Cherokee Rubicon

Although at first glance the Jeep Cherokee Rubicon may appear similar in some respects to a Camel Trophy Discovery, this much-modfied Jeep actually has many additional gadgets that the Camel Discovery lacks and vice versa. This does not necessarily make one vehicle better than the other; it is just that they have been designed to different parameters using alternative solutions to the same problems.

If one wanted to play devil's advocate, it could be said that the Rubicon is better suited to off-road trips in and around Europe, while the Camel Discovery has been purpose-built to cope with the demands placed on it by the long-distance expe-

*Fig.51 Featuring raised suspension and oversize tyres, the Jeep Cherokee Rubicon is ready for serious off-road adventure.*

ditionary nature of the Camel Trophy. Either way, there can be no doubt that both vehicles are excellent performers off-road, and the modifications made to both of them could equally be applied to any off-road vehicle.

Unlike the Camel Discovery (of which at least forty are manufactured each year for the Camel Trophy), the Cherokee Rubicon was built as a one-off by Chrysler Jeep UK to demonstrate how the Cherokee can be turned from a good off-roader into a great one. The brainchild of the company's off-road demonstration manager Barry Stallard, the vehicle was modified to his own specification from experience gained through his many years of off-road driving. Taking a turbo-diesel Jeep Cherokee as a base, Barry used the skills of off-road preparation specialists Chris Bashall

and Surrey Off Road to produce the vehicle, and the result is certainly formidable.

The Rubicon has been designed to be almost completely self-sufficient off-road with locking axle differentials, electric winches front and rear and oversized Mud-Terrain tyres providing the capability to get through (or at least get unstuck from) the most serious off-road obstacles imaginable. Surrey Off Road installed the vehicle's twin winches, the uprated electrical system and the hefty side protection bars that can also be used as jacking points for the interior mounted hi-lift jack. Like the Camel Discovery, additional lighting for night-time off-roading has also been incorporated, although in this case the roof-mounted lights are removable for on-road use. The lack of a roof rack also means that the vehicle handles better on-road and is capable of higher cruising speeds on the motorway.

Because there is no space for equipment storage outside the vehicle, the Rubicon has had its rear seat removed to create room for its comprehensive inventory of off-road equipment. As a result the vehicle is a two-seater, but with a little reorganization extra passengers could be carried. Unless you have a family, a driver and co-driver is all you need for most off-road forays.

To store all the off-road equipment, Jeep have chosen lightweight but strong plastic boxes, all of which are securely tied down in the back of the vehicle to prevent them

becoming dislodged over bumpy terrain. Likewise, heavy items like the hi-lift jack and Max Tool have their own lashings to keep them firmly in place when not required. Two spare wheels are also carried – a worthwhile investment should you be considering going off-road for long distances.

One of the main advantages the Rubicon has over the Camel Discovery is its locking axle differentials, which allow it to literally crawl over obstacles that would probably leave the Discovery stuck with its wheels spinning. As we explained in Chapter 2, permanent four-wheel drive systems require differential locks if they are to be true all-wheel drive vehicles in every sense. With open differentials power will always find the

*Fig.52 The Cherokee's front- and rear-mounted winches allow it to be entirely self-sufficient off-road.*

easiest way out, and that generally means the wheels with the least traction.

Below, we list the modifications and equipment carried in full.

*Suspension:*
This has been uprated and raised to accept the oversize tyres, give greater ground clearance and provide more axle articulation. Two additional dampers have been fitted to each axle, which allows them to share the load and provide useful back-up should one of the pair become damaged.

Front: Warn Black Diamond replacement coil springs. Four Black Diamond dampers (two each side).

Rear: Two Warn Black Diamond helper leaf springs fitted to the standard leaves. Four Black Diamond dampers (two each side).

*Wheels and Tyres:*
Standard Jeep Cherokee alloy wheels. Oversize BF Goodrich Mud-Terrain tyres (31/10.50 x 15s), which – together with the suspension modifications – give about three inches of lift.

*Additional Features, External:*
• Two Warn M8000 8,000lb electric winches – positioned front and rear of the vehicle. Having a winch at the back of the vehicle allows you to pull yourself back out of trouble. Invariably when you get stuck a front-mounted winch is facing the wrong way!
• Modified bumpers front and rear to accommodate the winches. They also incorporate two hi-lift jacking points at each end.
• Custom-made side sill protectors. These can also be used as a hi-lift jacking point.
• Two bumper-mounted driving lights.
• Two forward facing roof spotlights (removable).
• Two rearward facing roof spotlights (removable).

• Winch remote-control socket integrated into front decker panel.
• Flared wheel arches to accommodate wider tyres.
• Two front-mounted towing eyes
• One heavy-duty rear towing hitch. Incorporates towing ball.
• Full set of underside skid plates.
• Custom-made snorkel with remote axle and gearbox breathers.
• Plexiglass front light guards.

*Additional Features, Internal:*
• CB radio.
• Two rear-mounted spare wheels.
• ARB air locking axle differentials front and rear. Underbonnet compressor with air line.
• Two heavy-duty batteries with Warn split-charge system.
• Four lightweight equipment boxes (see below for inventory).
• Heavy-duty loadspace net with lashing eyes.
• Hi-lift jack (with wooden baseplate), sledgehammer, two Max tools (all securely tied down).
• Waterproof seat covers and floormats.
• Full first-aid kit.
• Fire extinguisher mounted in front passenger footwell.
• Large fire extinguisher mounted in near-side spare wheel.

*Equipment Carried:*
• Glove box: WD40.
• Centre cubby box: two pairs of work gloves, windscreen scraper, de-icer, magnetic warning beacon.
• Driver's door pocket: one pair of leather work gloves.
• Box one:
  – Two Max tool carry bags comprising: shovel head, mattock head, broad pick, chisel pick.
  – Two winch accessory kits comprising in

each: one tree strop, one shackle, one snatch block.
- Extension wire rope.
- One vehicle jack, handle and wheel-brace.
- One hi-lift extension bracket.
- One nylon sack (to cover winch wire rope)
- Two winch remote-control units.
- Box two:
  - Two front wiper blades.
  - 90 piece socket set.
  - One mallet
  - One box spare bulbs and fuses.
  - Spare air filter.
  - Spare oil filter.
  - One workshop manual.
  - Spare safety rope.
  - One set of jump leads.
  - Two heavy-duty ratchet straps.
- Box three:
  - One small bow saw.
  - Air line (for ARB compressor).
  - Air bag jack.
  - Large torch.
  - Five ratchet straps.
  - Canvas bag.
- Box four:
  - Four safety ropes with shackles.

- 1 x 60ft (18m) recovery rope.
- 1 x 15ft (4.5m) recovery rope.
- Two bridles with two shackles each.
- Tool boxes:
  - One junior hacksaw with spare blades.
  - Three small wire brushes.
  - One crimping tool kit with connectors.
  - One set of electricians' screwdrivers.
  - Two pairs of mole grips.
  - One set of tin snips.
  - 1 x 10in (25cm) adjustable spanner.
  - One plastic-faced hammer.
  - 2 x 24 piece combination spanner set.
  - Tube of Super Glue.
  - 16 piece screwdriver set.
  - One extended wheelbrace with socket.
  - Four rolls of insulation tape.
  - Eight cable ties.
  - Two centre punches.
  - One small chisel.
  - Two angled screwdrivers.
  - One pair side cutters.
  - One pair of long-nosed pliers.
  - One pair pliers.
  - One set of allen keys.
  - One round file.
  - One half-round/flat file.
  - Two screwdrivers.
- Cool box containing soft drinks and an ice pack!

# 4 Off-Roading: the Basics

## FINAL CHECKS AND PREPARATIONS

With the vehicle suitably equipped and ready for action there are a few last-minute checks that you should carry out before venturing off-road. Just as you would check the oil, tyre pressures and water level before undertaking a long journey on-road, it is even more important to give the vehicle a thorough going-over before leaving the tarmac. Although your average speeds off-road are likely to be a tenth or less of your speeds on-road, it is worth remembering that your vehicle will probably be working harder off the tarmac, thanks to more frequent gear changes, a reliance on engine braking and the obvious increased suspension movements.

As a result you should ensure that your vehicle is in top-notch condition; if it isn't, be prepared for a breakdown! Starting under the bonnet, check all the fluid levels (oil, water, clutch and brake fluid) and add the appropriate amount of each to bring them to their optimum levels. While under the bonnet check the HT leads, making sure that none is loose or worn. Similarly, ensure that the battery is securely tied/clamped down and if it needs topping up, do so. This is particularly important if you have a winch, as this takes a lot of current draw.

If you have a petrol engine and intend to go wading, it is important that you make some effort to waterproof your electrics — otherwise you risk stalling the engine, or at the very least causing a misfire while the engine dries itself out. Diesels do not have this problem, although you should always be aware of where the air intake is or, better still, fit a snorkel (see Chapter 3).

Waterproofing a petrol engine is a relatively straightforward process, although you will need some silicon grease and a can of silicon spray to do the job. These can be bought from specialist off-road equipment suppliers although they are also available from any electronics shop.

*Fig.53 Always check that your vehicle is in a fit state to go off-road before sallying forth.*

Starting with the distributor, unclip the cap and turn it around so that the underside is facing towards you. Taking the tube of silicon grease, carefully squeeze a thin ring around the inside of the cap taking care not to overdo it, and being careful not to smear any onto the metal contacts. After you have completely coated the inner circumference of the cap, smooth the grease out using your finger ensuring that there are no gaps. Replace the cap carefully making sure that none of the grease comes into contact with the rotor arm or contacts.

With the silicon spray, lightly spray the HT leads at the top of the distributor just enough to ensure that they have been completely covered. Work your way down the leads, making sure that each connection to the spark plug has also been lightly coated. After this, spray the coil and its leads, all of which should help repel water as it splashes up into the engine bay. Note that if you intend to go wading often, it is advisable to remount the coil high in the engine bay or even inside the cab. After this you should have very few problems when wading in really deep water.

Having finished under the bonnet, you need to give the rest of your vehicle a quick once-over to ensure that everything is as it should be. Check that your tyre pressures are correct and that your tyre walls are free from damage. Remember also to check that your spare is correctly inflated – you never know if you might need it! If your vehicle hasn't been serviced for a while, you might also like to check that the propshafts are well greased and that the wheel bearings are in order. Do this by placing a hand on each side of the tyre and trying to rock it from side to side. If there is excessive play, then it is likely that the wheel bearing needs replacing.

Finally (for those vehicles that have them) it is worth fitting the gearbox wading plug which normally screws in underneath the gearbox on the clutch housing. On Land Rover TDi models, there is an additional wading plug at the bottom of the timing chain cover which should also be fitted. Fitting a wading plug stops water from entering these breathing holes, although you should always remember to remove them once you get back onto the tarmac.

## INSIDE THE VEHICLE

Now that your vehicle is fully prepared to go off-road, you should take a look at the most important component: the driver. Unlike straight motorway driving, the majority of off-road situations require a great deal of arm and pedal movement, so it is important that you make yourself comfortable. Make sure that you can reach all the controls easily (even if your seatbelt is in the locked tension position) and that your seat is at the optimum position. If you have passengers make sure that they too are comfortable, that they are belted in and can also reach their own grab handles.

Although it may seem obvious, ensure that you are one hundred per cent familiar with the controls of your vehicle. We shall look at the various levers and buttons to use off-road in a later section, but you should instinctively know which controls operate items such as the windscreen wipers, demister vents and rear wash/wipe. If, for example, you hit a deep puddle at speed, water will cover the windscreen almost immediately and prevent you from seeing out. Knowing which button operates the windscreen wipers will allow you to be able to clear the windscreen as quickly as possible, thus restoring vision and maybe preventing you from ending up in a ditch!

Loose items inside the vehicle (such as tape boxes, map books, pens and de-icer) should be placed out of harm's way in the glove box or central cubby box, to prevent them from flying around the interior should they be dislodged as the vehicle sways from side to

*Fig.54 All your equipment should be well stored in the back of your vehicle. Use nets or sturdy straps to lash it down securely.*

side over undulating terrain. An unopened Coke tin can, from the author's own experience, prove very dangerous if it becomes wedged behind the clutch pedal, and removing it while driving off-road is extremely difficult indeed.

Heavier items (like your ropes, shackles and other recovery gear) should always be stored in the rear loadbay of your vehicle. Some off-roaders like to use robust plastic 'Action Packer' boxes to store their off-road gear, although the potential damage that such a box could do if it becomes dislodged during a roll-over does not bear thinking about. As such, always make sure that heavy items are tied securely to the vehicle floor, and that the vehicle's parcel shelf (if fitted) is in place to restrict any further movement. An additional safety precaution is the fitment of a mesh dog-guard between the load bay and the seating compartment. This makes sure that no object is likely to penetrate into the seating area and cause possible injury.

## CONTROLS AND WHAT THEY DO

Whereas the majority of controls in a 4x4 are similar to those of a 'normal' family saloon, there are one or two buttons and levers that are specifically designed for use off-road, and as such require some additional explanation.

Before proceeding, however, it is worth noting that few types of off-road vehicles are identical, and it is beyond the scope of this book to examine each vehicle individually. Instead, we shall offer a general guide to the different types of four-wheel drive system most commonly found in off-road vehicles. To make matters more complicated, some manufacturers use a slightly different system from others, and we shall try to accommodate these. We recommend that you read your owner's manual as a complement to this section and everything should then become clear.

## Selectable 4WD and Freewheeling Hubs (Series Land Rovers and Older 4x4s)

The selectable four-wheel drive set-up is without doubt the oldest four-wheel drive system, having its origins with the 1940 Willys/Bantam Jeep that is the great grand-daddy of all modern light 4x4s. For normal driving conditions (that is, on tarmac) the transmission supplies drive to the rear wheels only giving a 4x2 configuration, and with vehicles fitted with freewheeling hubs the front wheels 'freewheel' in the same way that all rear-wheel drive cars do. This offers more car-like roadholding and supposedly causes less wear to the front tyres and drive-train components, although this is likely to be minimal.

Naturally, 4x4 or all-wheel drive is prefer-able for off-road conditions and this is engaged by 'locking' the front axle hubs by turning the round disc located on them until the hubs 'click' into place. Although it is normal to leave the hubs in the 'free' position on-road, it is worth locking them to the '4x4' position as soon as you venture off-road. This ensures that full four-wheel drive is available as soon as you need it.

Remembering to lock and unlock the hubs for on-road/off-road use is very important, as the author's own experience has demon-strated. Having been used to a permanent four-wheel drive system, the author forgot to engage the hubs on a borrowed vehicle before venturing off-road and promptly became stuck. It was only after several attempts to get unstuck in two-wheel drive that he realized his error, finally getting out to lock them manually in position. Sure enough, with full four-wheel drive, the vehicle was able to crawl out of the mud under its own steam.

*Fig.55 Engage your freewheeling hubs before going off-road, as having to engage them in the mud is definitely not recommended!*

various parts of the transmission trying to work against each other. This is noticeable by a stiff feeling when the vehicle is turning, and can be released by reversing in a straight line.

## Permanent 4WD With Centre Differential Lock (Land Rover Defender/Discovery, etc)

This system has been in use by Land Rover since the launch of the Range Rover Classic in 1970, and – as its name suggests – it permanently transmits power to all four wheels thus giving maximum grip in all situations. However, the vehicle has to have a third differential in the gearbox to allow the front and rear axles to rotate at different speeds when the vehicle is turning on tarmac.

In theory this could allow power to be transmitted to just one wheel if all three differentials (ie: the pair in each axle and the third in the gearbox) are open and there is equal resistance on three of the wheels. In this sense, permanent four-wheel drive is relatively ineffective without having

*Fig.56 You should always select four-wheel drive before going off-road with a part-time system.*

## Part-time 4WD With Automatic Freewheel Hubs (Most Modern Japanese 4x4s)

This system is almost identical to the part-time four-wheel drive set-up, except that the vehicle locks its front wheel hubs automatically. Whenever low box is selected the hubs engage themselves, only releasing when high box is reselected. Occasionally you can hear a characteristic clicking sound as the hubs disengage.

It is especially important to ensure that this system is not engaged while on hard ground or tarmac, as it is especially susceptible to transmission 'wind-up' caused by the

*Fig.57 With the Land Rover permanent four-wheel drive system you have to lock the centre differential lock before going off-road.*

the centre differential locked. Remember that with all the differentials open the transmission will always supply power to the wheel or wheels with the least resistance.

Locking the centre differential allows power to be split equally between the front and rear axles thus ensuring that at least two wheels (that is, one on each axle) are supplying power at all times. In this sense it is a good idea to engage the centre differential lock as soon as your wheels leave tarmac, as there is little point using it once you are already stuck – especially where you would have been unlikely to get stuck with the differential locked!

As with the other four-wheel drive systems listed above, you should never drive on tarmac with the centre differential locked as transmission wind-up can occur. It is also worth noting that the vacuum system used by Land Rover on the Defender, Discovery and Range Rover Classic does not always disengage instantly when deselected. Don't worry if this is the case, as the system normally sorts itself out and switches off after a couple of hundred metres of tarmac driving.

## Permanent 4WD With Automatic Centre Differential Lock (Late-Model Range Rover)

In 1989 Land Rover fitted a new Borg Warner transfer box to the Range Rover Classic, which by means of a viscous coupling removed the need for the user to have to manually engage the centre differential lock. As such, this system is extremely straightforward to use – all you have to do is decide which gearbox ratio to use (see below) and let the vehicle do all the rest. The system has been carried over to the second generation Range Rover, so this is similarly easy to use off-road.

## The Transfer Box

Virtually every 4x4 off-road vehicle on the market (with the exception of the Toyota RAV4, Daihatsu Terios and Land Rover Freelander) has a high/low transfer gearbox, which effectively gives you two sets of gear ratios: a 'high' set for use on-road, and a 'low' set for off-road conditions. In almost every case the entire gear set of gear ratios (including reverse) is reduced by a ratio of almost 2:1, allowing greater control and the ability to make use of the engine's maximum torque for climbing steep gradients or for towing heavy loads.

Again, the way of selecting low ratio from high (and vice versa) differs according to each model, but in most cases the ratios are changed via a short lever situated near the main gearlever. To change from high into low, bring the vehicle to a standstill, depress the clutch and move the lever from the 'H' position through neutral into 'L'. If it proves a little tricky to select, engage second gear on the main gearbox and move the transfer lever into low while gently bringing the clutch up to the bite. You should find that it will lock into position quite easily using this method.

For automatics it is a similar procedure, although you should engage neutral ('N') on your gearbox before moving the transfer lever. If it proves difficult to select low, let the vehicle move forward slightly on the brakes and try again. You should find that moving the cogs slightly in this manner will make it easy to engage low box. Selecting high again from low is the reverse procedure in both cases.

Some more recent 4x4s (such as the new Range Rover, Ford Explorer and SsangYong Musso) have dispensed with the 'traditional' transfer box lever, instead making use of a dashboard-mounted electronic switch to select low box. You still need to select neutral and come to a standstill before engaging the different ratio, although the vehicle makes the change for you electronically.

In the case of the new Range Rover, the automatic version has a novel 'H'-gate gear selector with low range on the side furthest away from the driver. To change ratio, the driver simply moves the selector across to the left or right (according to the ratio required), and after waiting for the electronics to do their bit they then select the appropriate gear for the terrain. Could it be any easier?

## Steering, Brakes and Clutch

The final piece of information that the first-time off-roader should be aware of before venturing off-road for the first time is that the vehicle will feel completely different from how it does on tarmac. When off-road you really need to *drive* the vehicle, guiding it through each obstacle using the engine and steering much more than you would when on-road. As such, be aware at all times of your gear choice, the direction in which the front wheels are pointing and be careful not to ride the clutch. Try also to avoid using the brakes to slow the vehicle down, instead let the engine and the low ratio gears do all the work. Of course, there are times when you will have to use the brakes, but you should certainly find that you use them significantly less off-road than on-road.

If the ground conditions are muddy or slippery it is important to know which way the steering wheels are facing. In ruts it is not uncommon for the vehicle to continue straight ahead even when the steering wheels are facing hard left or right – remember that just because the steering wheel looks straight doesn't necessarily mean that the front wheels are also facing directly ahead. If in doubt, take a look out of the window to verify the actual direction of the front wheels.

*Fig.58 When driving off-road for the first time you will encounter a completely different set of sensations from your on-tarmac mileage.*

*Fig.59 Care must be taken with the Range Rover's rear overhang when traversing extreme terrain like this.*

In short, the experienced off-roader uses the throttle with great delicacy, rarely has need of the clutch and hardly ever uses the brake. He or she is also constantly aware of which direction the front wheels are pointing, and always uses them to best effect. The correct choice of gear, good use of steering and balanced throttle control are the keys to good off-roading.

### Approach, Departure and Ramp Break-Over Angles

It is important to know the limitations of your vehicle when travelling off-road, es-

pecially if bodywork damage is to be kept to a minimum. As the photograph demonstrates, a Range Rover has a longer rear overhang than a Land Rover Defender 90, and it is a similar story with the length of the wheelbase. Off-roaders term these as the approach, departure and ramp break-over angles, and these factors should be kept in mind when approaching (or leaving) hills, steep banks or humps.

A 4x4 with high approach and departure angles will be able to negotiate such obstacles without risk of dragging or scraping the bodywork or chassis along the ground, so it is worth being aware of your vehicle's limitations before attempting the impossible. Note also that extra accessories such as a nudge bar or low level tow hitch will affect the approach and departure angles of a vehicle quite drastically, and it may be worth removing them if you intend to do a lot of relatively serious off-roading. Bolt-on side-steps will also affect the ramp break-over angle, although they do offer a certain amount of protection to sills and door bottoms.

Owners with Range Rovers fitted with Land Rover's unique air suspension system may like to note that they can increase the approach and departure angles of their vehicle by raising the suspension to the 'high profile' mode. Although the ramp break-over angle is also increased, the amount is so small as to be insignificant.

### GENERAL OFF-ROAD DRIVING TECHNIQUES

As outlined above, a major part of successful and safe off-road driving lies in smooth and precise control of your vehicle through calculated use of the accelerator, gears and steering. At all times off-road you should be using your senses to feel how the vehicle is moving, and then react to this by operating

*Fig.60 The approach angle should be considered in the run up to steep hills. The spoiler reduces the approach angle quite significantly in this instance.*

*Fig.61 Bolt-on side steps reduce a vehicle's ramp break over angle.*

the major controls appropriately. As with most things in life there's no substitute for experience, and after a while you should become accustomed to the very different set of feelings you get when driving off-road. As such, it is important not to try to attempt the impossible when driving off-road for the first time – instead just get used to how the vehicle feels as it makes its way across the terrain. Once you are totally comfortable with this new driving experience you can try some more challenging tracks – but don't attempt to run before you can walk!

You will quite often see vehicles flying spectacularly through the mud and battling through obstacles at high speed in action off-road videos, but if you want to preserve your vehicle and avoid large repair bills this style of off-roading is to be avoided. Off-road guru David Bowyer has coined a phrase to describe the best way to drive off-road: 'Drive as slowly as possible and as fast as necessary.' In other words, if ground conditions demand momentum in order not to become stuck (deep, claggy mud for example), don't be afraid to use the throttle. However, if the tracks are relatively straightforward there's no need to overdo it – just potter along and enjoy the countryside.

As outlined above, correct gear choice is extremely important for safe and successful off-roading – but which gear and when? All 4x4 manufacturers spend vast amounts of money testing and perfecting their off-road vehicles' gearbox ratios, although the 'right' gear for the 'right' situation depends very much on the size of the vehicle's engine, the depth of the low range transfer gears and the engine's power and torque characteristics. For example, a situation requiring third gear low in a torquey V8 Range Rover will probably require second or even first gear low in a petite Suzuki 4x4 with a much smaller engine. To complicate matters further, there is a completely different set of rules for 4x4s fitted with an automatic gearbox!

Once again, experience will teach you

*Fig.62 The correct speed while off-road is crucial, but don't overdo it unnecessarily like this chap.*

*Fig.63 Smaller vehicles like the Suzuki SJ410 will require different gear choices from larger ones in similar off-road situations.*

which gear is the best for your vehicle and there are no hard and fast rules. The only exception to this is the use of first gear low for descending, which we shall discuss in more detail later on. In the case of vehicles fitted with an automatic gearbox, there is much debate as to the 'correct' gear for general use off-road. Although many off-roaders believe that you should keep the gearbox locked in third gear low while off-road, selecting 'drive' is equally acceptable. With an automatic, if you ever find a ratio too high you can either manually select a lower one or use the kickdown facility – off-roading in an automatic really is as straightforward as that.

When off-road you should constantly read the ground ahead, assessing forthcoming problems and mentally preparing the best course of action. Nevertheless, you should always have a back-up plan (or safety route) just in case. While driving off-road – especially in slippery, muddy conditions – what you would like to happen and what actually happens are often completely different! Never drive anywhere without knowing for sure what lies ahead, and never attempt to drive anything that you aren't entirely happy with – the experienced off-roader never takes chances. If ever you are in doubt, get out of the vehicle and check the route ahead on foot.

Two final pieces of advice that are worth remembering are: i) never have your thumbs

*Fig.64 While off-road you should constantly read the ground ahead. If you have any doubt as to what lies ahead, walk ahead to verify that it is drivable.*

hooked inside the steering wheel, and ii) remember to retract the radio aerial and close all windows. Although modern power-assisted 4WD vehicles tend to absorb most of the steering shocks when off-road, there are stories of people breaking their thumbs with a sudden sharp rotation of the steering wheel, so rest your thumbs on the rim.

Unless you are off-roading in the desert or in an area that has very few trees and sparse vegetation, the aerial should be retracted to prevent it becoming bent or snapped off by a rogue branch. Likewise, the windows should be almost completely shut to prevent branches or twigs entering the interior and potentially scratching your arm or – even worse – catching your eye and causing serious injury.

## MUD AND RUTS

All off-roaders seems to be irresistibly drawn to mud. Whether it is the basic desire to get

dirty or the enjoyment of driving on a slippery surface, off-roaders always seem to head for the biggest mud hole they can find and throw themselves and their vehicle into it.

Of all the obstacles you might encounter while off-road, mud would *appear* to be the least damaging, as being soft, it is unlikely to cause any panel damage. However, in actual fact mud is deceptively dangerous: its slippery surface can cause vehicles to slide out of control; the speed often required to get through a muddy section can place you and your vehicle at risk; while the abrasive consistency of mud can play havoc with vehicle brakes, wheel bearings and other moving components. As a result, mud should be treated with respect, even though it is relatively simple to drive.

Like ascending off-road, the best way to get through mud is to keep wheelspin to a minimum. As a result you should use the highest gear possible, keeping in mind the old adage: 'as fast as possible but as slowly as necessary'. If the mud section you are tack-

*Fig.65 Mud is deceptively dangerous, although most off-roaders seem irresistibly drawn to it!*

*Fig.66 Momentum is often the only way that you will be able to drive a muddy section without becoming stuck.*

ling has a relatively hard, stony base, you shouldn't need much momentum to get through; but if the mud is clay-based, power and momentum is the only option. Although not appropriate in every instance, full throttle in third gear low seems to work best with long mud runs. Remember that you should constantly be aware of the ground that you are approaching, thus allowing you to select the right gear and line of attack. If ever you are unsure, park your vehicle and have a look ahead on foot, and never be tempted to drive faster than your capabilities.

Another technique to assist you while driving through sticky mud is to rock the steering wheel from side to side in a seesaw motion, which consequently gives extra bite from the tyre sidewalls and the front wheels move in a similar fashion. Although this process may sound of little use on paper, moving the steering in such a manner is actually quite effective. Remember, though, when using this method to be aware of the direction of the front wheels and not to overdo it – if suddenly the vehicle gets traction and the wheels aren't straight, you'll tend to steer off course, which may mean off the track if you're not careful.

Even if you don't move the steering in a seesaw motion, you should still pay particular attention to the direction of the front wheels when driving in mud. Because mud and ruts tend to impair the steering, many drivers find themselves accidentally steering to the left or right while the vehicle continues to move forward, thus causing the vehicle to fight the intended direction of travel. This tramline effect is caused by ruts guiding the vehicle, and the best way to overcome it is to relax and hold the steering loosely in your palms – in effect let the vehicle steer itself (within reason). By feeling what the steering is doing, you can nearly always tell if the wheels are straight or not. If ever you are in doubt, stop the vehicle and stick your head out to have a look.

*Fig.67 Let ruts guide you if they're going in the right direction, although take care not to become high centred.*

Where a section of mud features ruts made by other vehicles let them guide you if they're going in the right direction. However when driving in ruts, make sure that they aren't too deep for your tyres, otherwise you may find yourself grounding out on the chassis and in need of recovery. Again, a fine balance of power and momentum will usually get you through, although if you do cease forward motion, try and reverse back and have another go with a little more gusto.

Before dropping into a set of ruts and committing yourself entirely, remember that once all four wheels are in the ruts it will probably be impossible to steer yourself out

Fig.68 *If ruts look deep, try to get out of them at the soonest possible opportunity.*

in. Like most off-road situations, you can only plan for so long – improvisation is a useful tool.

Ruts should also be straddled when they are formed from hard-baked mud. Apart from taking away complete control of the steering, the raised section of hard ground in between the ruts may cause damage to the underside of the vehicle; most notably the differential casings and transmission components if they are not adequately protected. Even if you don't cause any damage, you still risk becoming grounded on the hard centre – something that would have been so easy to avoid had you straddled the ruts in the first place.

of them. Constantly look for possible 'escape routes' just in case the ruts get too deep and you want to get out of them: a lower bank on one side of the rut, a tree root or a rock that could be used to give the wheel a little lift and some help in climbing out. If this doesn't work, only a hi-lift jack or winch will get you back out.

If the ruts look too deep to be driven without becoming stuck, try straddling them by placing a wheel on either side. With a little care the vehicle should stay on top, but if one set of wheels does drop in where the track is excessively slippery, keep moving. Those who hesitate risk becoming stuck, and the same applies if both sets of wheels drop

Fig.69 *Try to straddle ruts when they are deep or made from hard baked mud.*

# UNDULATING TERRAIN – CROSS AXLING AND CROSSING NARROW DITCHES

As we have discussed earlier, successful off-road driving requires constant awareness of the terrain around you and the subsequent application of technique to help you get through an obstacle. Reading the ground ahead, choosing the correct gear and deciding upon an appropriate amount of momentum are generally the keys to not becoming stuck, although there are a couple of situations where a full understanding of what might happen and how to deal with it is the best way to learn.

If you cast your mind back to the explanation of how four-wheel drive systems work in Chapter 2, understanding the principle of cross axling and why you get stuck should be quite straightforward. Cross axling is where diagonally opposed wheels become crossed and lose traction; that is to say the offside rear and nearside front wheels are at maximum suspension travel and as such have lost full contact with the ground. Because power will always find the easiest way out, the two wheels dangling in the air spin uselessly, while the wheels with traction remain stationary. In other words, you are stuck!

Apart from having an axle differential lock to share power equally between both wheels, there is only one way to avoid this situation, and that is to use momentum to carry you through. Often when a vehicle becomes cross

*Fig.70 Once you become cross axled in slippery conditions you are likely to become stuck. Only momentum will get you through without needing to use a winch or having a tow.*

*Fig.71 Don't try to drive a ditch straight on or you risk grounding your front bumper . . .*

*Fig.72 . . . instead, use the tried and trusted 1-2-3-4 diagonal approach shown here.*

axled it is possible to reverse back off the obstacle and give it another go. It is difficult to judge exactly how much momentum will be required for a given obstacle, but if you see an obstacle where cross axling may occur, don't be shy with the throttle. As always, don't overdo it, but drive too slow and you will grind to a halt and probably need recovering.

Crossing narrow ditches or relatively deep ruts also requires a specific technique if you and the vehicle are not to become stuck. The tendency for the first time off-roader is to approach the ditch head on, with the rather inevitable result that both front wheels drop into the hole at the same time, resulting in the front bumper becoming buried in the ground on the other side and one stuck vehicle.

To prevent this from happening, cross the ditch diagonally at an angle of approximately 45 degrees, allowing each wheel to drop into the ditch individually in a 1-2-3-4 manner (see diagram). This way you always have at least three wheels at the top of the ditch to provide enough traction to carry the vehicle through. Be aware though that this technique only works with moderately narrow ditches – crossing anything which would swallow a whole tyre should obviously be avoided!

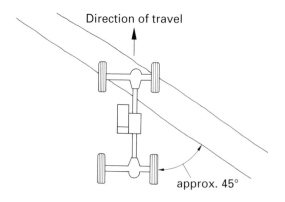

*Fig.73 Diagram of how to cross a ditch.*

The speed with which you cross the ditch is a final important consideration. Too slow and you risk becoming stuck with one wheel in the ditch; too fast and the vehicle may well lurch out of control or even roll over! First gear low will enable you to crawl into the ditch slowly, as well as offering a good dose of torque should you need to accelerate out of trouble. Even so, the low gearing of first low will prevent you from accelerating too much, thus preventing any surprise jumps or excessive lurching.

## HILL CLIMBS/DESCENTS

Sooner or later when driving off-road you will encounter a reasonably steep hill, and before attempting it you should be aware that hill climbing is one of the most hazardous areas of off-roading. Get it wrong and you could quite easily come rolling back down out of control, or – even worse – you might find yourself facing broadside on the hill. In this situation little, apart from luck, will stop you from rolling over and ending up in a crumpled heap at the bottom.

That said, with the right knowledge hill climbing is relatively straightforward – you just need to be aware of the failed hill climb technique to bring you safely back down to the bottom of the hill should you fail on your first attempt. The failed hill climb procedure is perhaps the most important technique in the off-roader's armoury, and we shall look at the theory in detail later in this section.

### Going Up

Before attempting to climb a hill, you must be sure of what lies on the other side. Hill climbing generally requires a good deal of momentum, and as you are often driving blind as you reach the summit you need to be confident of what lies ahead. If you are in any

*Fig.74 Before climbing a hill make sure that you know what lies on the other side . . .*

doubt leave the vehicle at the bottom of the hill, get out and walk to the top to check that the route ahead is clear. If the hill immediately drops back off again, you will need to stop at the top once you have climbed it and use the techniques outlined in the 'Coming Down' section. If this is the case and you weren't aware of it serious damage may result.

Once you are happy that the hill can be climbed successfully, you will need to select the right gear to complete the hill in one. It is simply not possible to change down a gear during the climb with a manual gearbox, and you should never attempt this even if the engine feels as though it is about to stall. If it

does, don't worry – let the vehicle come to a halt and use the failed hill climb to get you back down.

For most medium or large-sized 4x4s, second gear low is the best gear with which to tackle climbs. However, larger engined vehicles (those fitted with large capacity V8s for example) may be able to use third gear low, and some smaller-engined vehicles (little Suzukis or early petrol-engined Daihatsus) may require first gear low. Nevertheless, second low is perfect for the majority of vehicles.

The key to a successful hill climb is to balance the amount of speed required with the severity of the ascent, although ground conditions will also play a role here. For relatively dry 'grippy' ascents, you will probably be able to drive up gently using only a slight amount of throttle; while hills covered with slippery mud will need more momentum and possibly a higher gear to prevent excessive wheelspin. Once again there's no substitute for experience, and after a few attempts you should be able to 'feel' just how much power you require to make a successful climb.

Starting at the base of the slope, build up the vehicle's speed to the right amount for the climb. Grip the steering wheel relatively tightly in the straight ahead position and guide the vehicle up the slope. Be prepared for the vehicle to lurch from side to side if the going is rough, but remember to keep steering up the hill at all times. One exception to this rule is if the hill is relatively slippery. In this case, you may like to rock the steering backwards and forwards in a seesaw motion to help the tyres bite into the mud. Be careful not to overdo it, however, as the last thing you want to do is steer the vehicle off line!

Assuming that the climb is going well, as you reach the top of the slope start to let up on the throttle to allow the vehicle to come to a halt at the summit. As you checked this on foot to ensure that it is safe to proceed, you

*Fig.75  Don't use too much power when climbing hills, otherwise you risk lifting your front wheels and losing traction like this.*

*Fig.76  In slippery conditions, only momentum will help you climb the slope without becoming stuck.*

can now carry on with the next part of the track.

For vehicles fitted with an automatic gearbox, the procedure for hill climbing is identical with one exception: gear choice. As you don't have to change gear using the clutch, off-roaders fitted with an automatic gearbox are especially effective when climbing hills. Whereas it is almost impossible to change gear in mid-climb without losing momentum with a manual gearbox, with an automatic all you have to do is kick-down and the vehicle selects a lower ratio without losing speed.

Therefore, when hill climbing in an automatic, we recommend starting at the bottom of the hill with the gearbox locked in third gear low. This allows you to use the highest gear possible to prevent wheelspin, yet also gives you the option of kicking down to second should the hill prove to be more diffi-

cult. Should the hill still prove too steep at that speed and you come to a halt with your wheels spinning, the technique for a failed hill climb is easy to execute too (see below).

## Coming Down

Without intending to state the obvious, descending slopes requires a completely different style of driving from climbing them. Whereas momentum is often the only way to climb a hill, speed is positively discouraged when you are coming back down – instead you want to descend as gently as gravity will allow. As with most off-road techniques, forget everything about coming down steep slopes on tarmac (using the brakes for example), as the conditions encountered off-road require a completely different approach.

*Fig.77 Maximum engine braking can be obtained by selecting first gear low, and this should be used for all descents.*

Put simply, you should never use the foot-brake when coming down a hill off-road. Instead, rely on the vehicle's engine braking to control the rate of descent. One exception to this rule is 'power braking' with vehicles fitted with automatic transmission, but we shall cover this later in this section.

Maximum engine braking for all off-road vehicles is obtained with first gear low range – the lowest ratio in your gearbox. Therefore, all descents should be taken in first gear low, even if they appear relatively modest. If you do find first gear on tickover too slow, then accelerate the revs in this gear. Never be tempted to change gear while coming down a slope – as soon as you engage neutral then there is a possibility that gravity will take over and you will career down to the bottom completely out of control. When coming downhill you want as much control over your speed as possible.

Having ensured that first gear low is selected, gently apply the throttle to ease the vehicle over the edge of the descent. You can now take your feet off all the pedals and let the vehicle do all the hard work, while you concentrate on keeping the steering straight ahead. Be careful not to ride the clutch as you descend, as a sudden jolt may make you depress the clutch thus throwing the vehicle into neutral, which could result in total loss of control.

The above technique works for the majority of cases, although if the slope is particularly slippery first low on tickover may be too low, and the vehicle will start to slide. If this happens don't jam on the brakes as this will make the situation much worse. Instead gently depress the throttle to allow the wheels to 'catch up' with the speed of the vehicle, which will then allow you to regain control once again. If you can, back off on the throttle again to slow the vehicle down, but if the wheels start sliding again repeat the above procedure. If you can't regain control once more, then the slope is far too steep and you should never have attempted it in the first place!

As we mentioned earlier, you should never use the brakes when descending, as the wheels will lock up and you will slide out of control to the bottom. But, due to the

*Fig.78 Remember to steer straight ahead when descending, unless of course the track requires otherwise.*

*Fig.79 If you fail a hill, reverse straight back down using the failed hill climb procedure.*

mechanical make-up of the automatic gearbox, off-road vehicles fitted with clutch-less transmission systems tend to have less engine braking than equivalent engined vehicles with a manual transmission. For most situations the level of engine braking offered by an automatic gearbox is perfectly safe – you just end up at the bottom of the hill going slightly faster than you would do in an equivalent manual model. However, for particularly steep descents this can be dangerous, and in this case you should think about using the technique of 'power braking'.

Put simply, power braking allows you to apply the brakes while going downhill but still remain in control. You do this by braking with your left foot, but at the same time applying some throttle with your right one to counteract the stopping effect of the brakes. Such a technique takes some practice to perfect, and you might like to try it on a reasonably modest descent before attempting something a little more tricky.

Some manufacturers suggest that their ABS systems can also be used to slow down a vehicle on a steep descent, but as this tech-nique is by no means clear-cut we recommend that you disregard this piece of information until you are sufficiently experienced to cope with a possible slide downhill!

One final word about engine braking: it is worth noting that the high compression ratios of most diesel engines will result in greater engine braking when coming down-hill in comparison with their petrol equivalents. This is useful, but shouldn't necessarily encourage you to attempt coming downhill in second gear low, even if it does feel slow in first. Selecting first gear low is always the safest way to come downhill.

## The Failed Hill Climb Procedure

As we mentioned earlier, the failed hill climb procedure is probably the most important technique for the off-roader to know. With a vehicle unable to go anywhere but down in the middle of a slope it is potentially a very dangerous situation to be in, and you will want to get back down to the bottom in the most controlled way possible.

Let's assume that the vehicle is still running, but the wheels are spinning and you're going nowhere. To halt the vehicle on the slope, push the footbrake down hard while at the same time engaging the clutch to stop drive from being transmitted to the axles. The vehicle should remain stationary on the slope with the footbrake applied, giving you a chance to select reverse ready to drive back down. Assuming that your wheels are facing straight ahead, place your right hand at the top of the steering wheel at the twelve o'clock position. Doing this will allow you to turn around to see out of the back of the vehicle, at the same time ensuring that your front wheels remain straight ahead for the duration of the descent. Turning the wheel even slightly off centre may drag your vehicle's heavy front end round diagonally to the slope, which could result in disaster.

With your steering taken care of, release the clutch and brake simultaneously to engage reverse low, and gently come back down under engine braking. As with going downhill forwards, take your feet off all the pedals and let the vehicle do all the work. It is advisable to bring the clutch just up to the bite before releasing the footbrake completely, as this will ensure that reverse gear is correctly selected. Once you are back down at the bottom, think why you failed the climb and prepare yourself for another go!

If you stall the vehicle on the ascent (a common problem if the gear selected is too high for the engine's torque), the failed hill climb technique is exactly the same, with the exception of the use of the clutch. Hold the vehicle on the footbrake as before and select reverse in the normal manner,

however this time release the clutch again so that the vehicle is in gear while the engine is still switched off. Try releasing the footbrake gently to see if the engine will hold itself on the hill, but do be prepared for a slight movement backwards as any slack in the transmission is worked out. With the footbrake now completely off, flick the ignition key so that the engine starts in gear, but remember to place your hand at the twelve o'clock position to keep the front wheels straight. You'll experience a lurch as the engine fires, but the engine braking in low range reverse will take the vehicle back down under complete control.

As there is no clutch to worry about on 4x4s fitted with an automatic transmission, failed hill climbs are slightly more straightforward. Hold the vehicle stationary on the slope with the footbrake and select reverse low with the gearbox selector, taking care to ensure that the reverse has indeed been selected. You can then release the footbrake and let the vehicle come down under engine braking. As with all automatics, the amount of engine braking will be less than a 4x4 with manual transmission, so you might like to consider power braking if the slope is particularly steep (see above). It should be noted, however, that power braking in reverse is quite a tricky operation, so you should avoid it whenever possible.

Stalling a 4x4 with an automatic gearbox is virtually impossible (it may occur with older vehicles with badly tuned engines or a defective ECU), so you are unlikely to have to carry out a failed hill climb with the engine switched off. If your automatic vehicle does stall however, you will be unable to start the engine in gear as you would with a manual transmission due to the mechanical make up of the gearbox. Instead hold the vehicle stationary with the footbrake, select neutral and start the engine. With the engine running again, continue with the failed hill climb procedure as above.

# WATER WADING

Water (particularly deep water!) seems to have an irresistible draw for off-roaders, although wading can be treacherous if not done properly, with the potential for serious engine damage constantly present. As such, the best advice we can give when approaching water is to avoid it wherever possible, and if it is unavoidable treat it with respect and extreme caution. In this chapter we shall look at wading in a standard, relatively unprepared vehicle – the next chapter covering advanced off-road techniques will look at driving through water above the manufacturer's recommended wading limit, although in this case some modifications are required to the vehicle.

Most 4x4 manufacturers set a maximum wading limit of around 50 centimetres (19.5 inches), which is normally about a thumb's length below the top of the wheel rim. With care this level can be slightly exceeded, although you should be very aware of exactly where the vehicle's air intake is situated. Sucking water into the air intake will cause the engine to hydraulic, resulting in bent con rods, a broken vehicle and a very large repair bill indeed.

As a result, you should always ascertain exactly how deep the water you intend to wade is. This is best done by walking ahead using rubber waders and a large stick to poke around underneath the surface of the water. With large areas of water, make sure that you probe the base in a large enough area to

*Fig.80 Always ascertain how deep the water is before driving in . . .*

*Fig.81  Always drive slowly into the water.*

*Fig.82  You must judge how much momentum to use to create the perfect bow wave, thus keeping the water out of the engine compartment.*

ensure that there are no hidden dips or muddy patches that could trap the unwary. Be extremely thorough with this on-foot recce, as muddy water can hide all sorts of nasty traps. The author once became stuck in a seemingly innocuous looking pool, which had a quicksand-like base caused by others spinning their wheels and churning up the silt at the bottom. Ironically, the same stretch of water had been driven clean only ten days earlier – it just goes to show that there's no substitute for checking and rechecking that the route ahead is safe to drive.

With this in mind, remember that deep mud underneath the water will cause wheels to sink further, and serious traction problems may then be encountered. Whereas momentum will carry you through exposed mud, there is a limit to how fast you can go when the mud is submerged underneath two feet of water.

Once you are convinced that it is safe to proceed, select second gear low and slowly dip the nose into the water. Advance slowly into the water on tickover, but once the rear wheels have dropped in, gently apply some power to push the vehicle forwards with enough momentum to create a modest bow wave in front of the front bumper. This has the effect of producing a compression curve below the bumper, thus pushing water away from the front of the engine and the fan. Judging the correct speed to do this is some-

*Fig.83 Too much speed and you risk drowning the engine.*

thing that requires some experience – just remember to keep things smooth and controlled.

If the vehicle stalls in the water (through badly protected electrics or the wrong gear choice), don't panic! However, do get the engine started again as quickly as possible, as the vacuum left by the cylinders' compression can suck water up through the exhaust pipe and cause serious damage. More often than not the engine will restart with a little gentle persuasion, but if it doesn't, wind the vehicle onto dry ground using the starter motor with first gear low engaged. You can then sort the problem out in safety.

Fording rivers requires a similar tech-nique, although you should always ensure that you have a suitable exit point in mind before sallying forth. Avoid fast flowing rivers at all times, as there is a very real danger that you will be swept away with the current. On the Camel Trophy they overcome this by wedging open the doors to sink the vehicle down to make contact with the riverbed. Nevertheless, unless you are prepared to put up with wet carpets and a sodden interior, this is not a technique that comes highly recommended! With rivers, remember that still waters run deep – avoid such areas at all costs.

When crossing relatively shallow rocky stream beds, it is worth selecting first gear low to really pick your way through the rocks

*Fig.84 When crossing a rocky stream bed, it is worth having some spotters walking ahead to check the route.*

on tickover. Providing that you aren't riding the clutch and the rocks aren't too big, tickover will be enough to pull you through at a slow crawl. However, be prepared to stop suddenly if you see a rock that might cause damage to the underside of the vehicle or puncture the differential casing. If large rocks are submerged, get someone to walk ahead to guide you through safely.

## AFTER AN OFF-ROAD SESSION

Before going back onto public roads, clean the vehicle of mud as much as possible, paying particular attention to clogged up tyres. Without cleaning the lugs, large amounts of mud will fly off your tyres as soon as you hit a reasonable speed on the tarmac,

causing a mess and potential hazard for other road users. Although this might not be too much of a problem with only one vehicle, if you multiply this by a factor of six to take into account other vehicles in an off-road convoy, then the amount of mud left behind will be considerable.

Other areas to check immediately before driving on tarmac are the vehicle's lights and number plates. If you have been driving through mud (normally the case when off-roading in the UK!), you will need to ensure that all the indicators, brake lights, rear lights and headlights are free from dirt and totally clean. Both the front and rear number plates should also be mud-free, so it is well worth having a clean piece of rag or some paper towels with which to clean them.

Having partially obscured or dirty lights and/or number plates while on a public highway is an offence, and you are likely to be pulled over by the police if you forget to clean them off before driving off on the road.

Another important thing to do before driving off at high speed is to give the vehicle a quick visual check. This is something that is often overlooked by many off-roaders in their hurry to get home after a tiring day's off-roading. Nevertheless this visual check is extremely important, as your vehicle could have sustained all sorts of damage during your off-road session; something that might only manifest itself at relatively high road speeds. Key areas to check are the brake lines, suspension, steering components and the wheels and tyres as well as the usual fluid checks under the bonnet. Check the bodywork also for damage and foliage – something that is especially important if you have a roof-rack. The author once drove for six miles with a significant branch securely lodged in his roof-rack after forgetting to

check for debris before setting off on the tarmac.

As soon as you can, hose the vehicle down using a pressure washer. Although it might be a excellent fun posing in town in your normally shiny off-roader, mud, sand and even dust will wear mechanical components extremely quickly. Remember not just to limit your attention to the outside of the vehicle and the bits underneath that are easy to reach.

To do a really thorough job with a pressure washer, you should be prepared to spend at least twenty minutes hosing all areas of the vehicle, including the engine compartment, chassis and transmission components situated right underneath the vehicle. One area that needs particular attention – especially if you have been driving in deep and claggy mud – is the radiator and vehicle cooling system. Always hose this from the inside out at low pressure, so that the delicate cooling fins aren't damaged or bent back. We've seen vehicles overheat that haven't been cleaned off properly.

*Fig.85 Check over your vehicle after an off-road session, otherwise you might risk driving off with a branch on your roof as has happened here.*

# 5 Off-Roading: Advanced

As your confidence off-road increases and your horizons expand, you will find yourself venturing further and further afield in search of off-tarmac adventure. However, it is important to be fully confident in your own capabilities and those of your vehicle before tackling really serious tracks. Confidence comes with experience, so this chapter aims to help you learn the correct techniques to take on more serious obstacles safely and without fear.

## LARGE ROCKS AND DIFFICULT TRACKS

Rocks and stones demand greater care to drive than may at first be realized. Larger rocks that are virtually unmovable can all too easily cause damage to the vehicle's over-hangs and underside if you aren't careful and fully aware of the dimensions of your vehicle, while rocky tracks consisting of small stones can be deceptively tricky. As well as the

*Fig.86 Rocks and stones demand greater care to drive than may at first be realized.*

*Fig.87 When the terrain is extremely rocky, use an extra set of eyes to 'spot' the vehicle through.*

obvious damage that can be caused by flying stones coming into contact with the bodywork and underside, tyres are also at risk. The author has suffered from a number of punctures while off-road, including a spectacular blow-out caused by an extremely small flint rupturing the sidewall of a virtually brand-new tyre. The expensive tyre was irreparable and had to be thrown away, so great care should be taken when off-roading over shale-covered ground.

A common mistake when driving over flint-surfaced tracks is excessive speed. Although most of these types of track are deceptively smooth inside the vehicle, underneath, your suspension components and tyres are probably going through an ordeal.

As such you should stick to third gear low to keep speed down. Another problem is the unpredictable nature of the small stone surface, caused by the way that loose stones move over each other. With a really deep layer of stones, your ability to brake and steer is seriously impaired, so you may find yourself hurtling off the track unexpectedly. In this case, try to avoid wide throttle openings and using the brakes. Instead, use the gears to slow yourself down, as you should do at all times off-road.

As we mentioned in Chapter 4, you should be constantly reading the ground ahead and anticipating your next move when off-road. With rocky tracks this is especially important, as you may suddenly come across large potholes, rocks or deep water in the middle of the track representing sudden danger. If you are driving too fast, you might be unable to take avoiding action.

On tracks consisting of large rocks and boulders, extreme caution should be taken if body and underside damage is to be avoided. The key to a successful passage is to be certain that you are taking the least punishing route, and it is rare that you can judge this for yourself from the driving seat. This extremely precise form of off-roading requires a second set of eyes outside the vehicle to guide you carefully over the obstacle. Make sure that your assistant checks both the bodywork and underside of the vehicle for potentially damaging rocks as you make your way forward. This should be

done in first gear low for absolute control, and your foot should never be too far away from the footbrake. In situations like this, vehicles fitted with automatic transmission have a natural advantage!

When traversing a track covered with large rocks, constantly be aware of the potential for being thrown off course by a rock under the wheels. On vehicles fitted with all-smoothing coil suspension this isn't too much of a problem, but with leaf springs and some independent set-ups, this can result in the whole vehicle being thrown to one side. If you happen to be in a narrow gully at the time this may be slightly inconvenient. Remember too to keep a watch out for any rocks that could puncture the sidewall of a tyre.

On rutted tracks with a rocky centre be

*Fig.88 Drive slowly using first gear low to really pick your way across rocky terrain.*

very aware of large rocks and/or indentations where preceding vehicles have scraped their differentials along the ground. Scraping your differential or axles along such exposed rocks is extremely hazardous indeed, as you could very easily puncture the metal casing and drop all the oil. Apart from the environmental impact of spilt oil, you would be unable to run the vehicle with a dry differential. The author has heard of an emergency repair using a large quantity of chewing gum to plug the hole and some crushed bananas serving as lubricant in the axle – but this option should only be used in an absolute emergency! Instead, it's better to straddle any suspect ruts if it is feasible and safe to do so; or you could think about moving particularly risky rocks to one side of the track.

Ascending and descending on rocky tracks requires a different approach from normal hills. Whereas momentum is often the only way to get to the top of a muddy slope, on rocky tracks with a firm base you want to pick your way up the hill as slowly as possible to avoid too much lurching from side to side and the potential for damage. As such, you will probably want to use first gear low on tickover to make your way up the slope, being careful – as always – not to ride the clutch. Rocky ascents normally offer a staggering amount of grip, so you should have no fears about not making it to the top. Likewise, most off-road vehicles have a lot of low down torque, so it is unlikely that you will stall, even on tickover. If you do, just use the failed hill climb technique as outlined in Chapter 4.

If you have to climb slopes with a loose shale surface, use second or third low as you would with a muddy incline, but with less throttle as suggested in Chapter 4. If you lose grip and your wheels start to spin, stop immediately, otherwise you will just dig yourself in and find it hard to reverse back down for a second attempt. Remember, the

*Fig.89 Coming down rocky descents requires a lot of care and some judicious use of the brake.*

more aggressive your tyre tread pattern, the quicker you will dig a hole in the loose rock surface.

Coming down rocky descents also requires a lot of care, once again thanks to the ever-present danger of being thrown off course by a particularly large rock. As with all descents, you should drive down the slope in first gear low range for the utmost control, keeping an eye on the steering and the track ahead. With descents on loose rock, you may like to consider opening the throttle a little more to prevent the possibility of the wheels locking up on the slippery surface. Once again however, first gear low should be used, and the brakes should be left alone.

*Fig.90 Try to avoid locking the wheels when descending over loose rocks.*

*Fig.91 The key to driving a V-gully is keeping the vehicle level. Use an extra pair of eyes to keep the wheels pointing in the right direction.*

# V-GULLYS

When off-roading in open moorland or other areas with a high rainfall you will find that tracks featuring V-gullys are quite commonplace. As its name suggests, the V-gully is a section of track that has become eroded by water over the years, eventually resulting in the formation of a V shape which has to be traversed. If a lot of rain has fallen recently, you will often find a small stream running at the bottom of the gully continuing the erosion process.

The key to successfully driving a V-gully is to constantly keep the vehicle as level as possible, even if this means that you are running on the sidewalls of your tyres. Under no circumstances be tempted to drive with

*Fig.92 You will often be sitting on the tyre sidewalls when traversing a V-gully.*

one wheel higher than the other, as it is likely that you will slip down into the gully and either get stuck or have to proceed with one side of the body scraping along the gully wall. Not recommended if you want to avoid damaging the bodywork.

Although keeping the vehicle level in a V-gully sounds easy in theory, such a technique is actually quite difficult to master, largely because you will probably be running with very little tyre tread actually in contact with the ground. In every case, walk the gully beforehand and plan your route. Once this has been done, drive slowly ahead in first gear low (second low if the gully features a slight ascent), and if you have a co-driver get them to guide you through the obstacle from outside the vehicle. They will be able to see the front tyres on the gully walls, ensuring that they are pointing in the best direction to keep the vehicle level.

If ever it seems as though the vehicle is about to slip down, or if it appears impossible to keep the vehicle level, reverse out of the gully and seek an alternative route.

## BOGS AND DEEP MUD

The first thing that you should be aware of about mud is that it can damage your vehicle more than you might think. The abrasive qualities of the gooey brown stuff will soon wear suspension bushes, transmission joints, brakes and brake pads. Although mud is great fun to play in, if you want to preserve your vehicle, avoid it at all costs!

Nevertheless, if you're going off-road there's no doubt that you will encounter mud at some point during your journey, and in this section we will look at the best ways to tackle it without becoming stuck. It should be noted, however, that for really muddy sections the standard road-biased tyres fitted as standard to most off-road vehicles will prove extremely disadvantageous when it

*Fig.93 Although mud will seldom cause panel damage, really deep mud will wear down suspension components very quickly.*

*Fig.94 You'll need to use momentum to get through really boggy terrain . . .*

*Fig.95 . . . although sometimes there's only so much you can do.*

comes to really gooey mud. Even vehicles fitted with aggressive bar-type off-road tyres may have problems in this situation, so you must make sure that the tyres you have on your vehicle are suitable for the type of terrain you wish to tackle (see Chapter 2).

Put simply, there's only one way to deal with a particularly muddy track, and that's to use momentum. As we discussed in Chapter 4, you should always be looking ahead at the track in front of you, and with a little experience you should be able to ascertain how serious the ground conditions are ahead. With this knowledge, you can then select the right gear for the job and also

gauge how much momentum you will need to get you through without becoming stuck. At all times assess the ground conditions ahead of you – a track that can be gently driven in second at tickover in the dry may need full throttle third gear when it is really wet. Don't be shy with the throttle, but do make sure that it is safe to blast through before committing yourself entirely.

If the muddy track has ruts that don't look as if they will high centre your vehicle, use them to keep the vehicle on course – in this case, you will only need to keep a light pressure on the steering wheel. It is very unlikely that you will fly out of the ruts, so you can use a good dose of power to drive through the mud. If there aren't any ruts, be a little more cautious with the throttle and keep a firm hold of the steering – the last thing you want to do is speed off the track into the undergrowth! If the track is quite waterlogged, switch the windscreen wipers on before you drive off.

One of the best pieces of advice for successful mud driving is to relax. Grip the steering wheel firmly, but at the same time don't fight it as the front wheels make their way through the ruts. As with muddy inclines, you may like to rock the steering wheel back and forth in a seesaw motion to gain extra traction. As the front wheels move from side to side, the shoulder lugs on the side of the tyres make contact with the side of a rut, and the effect this can have on traction is astounding.

As you would with all off-road tracks, pick your route carefully bearing in mind the conditions, and the capability of you and your vehicle. On Camel Trophy Kalimantan '96 (arguably one of the toughest Trophies ever), it was interesting to see the difference that route choice made for identical Camel Trophy Discoverys tackling the same muddy sections. Some teams decided to drive straight ahead through the ruts and invariably got stuck, while others took a less obvious route around to the side of the sticky patch, making it through clean with very little momentum indeed. Experience will teach you which route looks the most promising.

Unless you really have to drive across deep bogs (such as those found in certain moorland areas of Wales), try to avoid them if you can. You can only normally drive deep boggy sections clean when it is dry, and during the winter months it is rare to be able to drive them without becoming horrendously stuck. Once you are sunk axle-deep in a bog, only a long and laborious recovery will get you going again.

Like most muddy tracks, bogs require a good dose of welly to get you through – he or she who hesitates will probably become stuck. Although speeding through bogs looks spectacular with mud and water flying all over the place, you are actually causing less damage by driving through quickly than if you tried the same track slowly and had to spin your wheels as you inevitably become stuck. It is important at this stage to stress the environmental impact of driving bogs, as the soft ground surface quickly deteriorates after being driven. Wherever possible, try and stick to firm ground around the bog, although be careful not to stray away from the legal right of way. Farmers can understandably become upset with off-road vehicles wandering onto their sensitive grazing land.

*Fig.96 If you do get stuck in mud, a long recovery and a lot of digging is often necessary to get yourself out.*

*Fig.97 Never try wading really deep water if your vehicle isn't prepared for it. This Suzuki's engine had to be completely rebuilt after it took in water.*

For really deep bogs, letting down your tyre pressures may give extra assistance, as the deflated tyre leaves a bigger print and gives a little extra flotation. A pressure of around 15psi is about right for most off-road vehicles but, before letting your tyres down, make sure that you have the means to re-inflate them before you get back on the road. Running your tyres below their recommended pressure on tarmac is inadvisable and dangerous, especially if you will be travelling at high speed once you get back on the road.

Another way to achieve extra flotation when crossing bogs is to use aluminium sand ladders as a makeshift 'bridge', creating a type of 'floating roadway'. To do this however, you will need a fair number of sand ladders which will have to be rotated from back to front as the vehicle makes its way across. This method of crossing a bog is fairly labour intensive and not guaranteed to work, and you may have a lot of problems rescuing a sunken ladder from underneath a vehicle should the vehicle's weight prove too much. Moving forward across a misplaced ladder could cause damage to the axles or brake pipes. If you do become stuck in a bog, see the section on how to recover your vehicle in Chapter 6.

## DEEP WATER WADING

As we mentioned in Chapter 4, the maximum wading limit set by most 4x4 manufacturers is around 50cm (19in), and although this can be exceeded in standard vehicles with a little care, we don't recommend taking to any really deep water unless you have a high-level air intake and a properly prepared vehicle. Remember though, that the bolt-on raised air intake must be completely sealed, otherwise you risk taking in water and completely destroying your engine. Just one loose jubilee clip on the air inlet could be

*Fig.98 If the water is really deep, you may need to open the vehicle's doors to prevent it floating and losing traction.*

enough to let in water – if you intend to go deep water wading, do make sure that your snorkel and its connections are in tip-top condition.

As well as the engine air intake, the gearbox and axles also need to breathe when going deep water wading. On modern Land Rover products, remote breathing tubes are positioned high in the engine bay, but if you're going wading above the recommended depth, you'll probably need to extend these up higher – probably up the side of the high level intake as they are with Camel Trophy vehicles. If you don't, water can be drawn inwards as axle and engine components cool in cold water, resulting in possible damage as water mixes with oil.

Although the water is deep, the normal wading procedure applies; that is to say,

second gear low range should be selected and you should enter the water smoothly, creating a bow wave in front of the vehicle. Since the water is deep your headlights should be switched off, as the shock of cold water could possibly crack the lenses. Similarly, after you have left the water, check that the headlights do not have any water inside them. If they do, you will have to remove them and drain it out. Water inside the lights will most definitely crack the bulbs almost as soon as they are switched on.

If you are wading in water that comes above the bottom of the doors, be prepared for leaks. Door seals are simply not designed to be one hundred per cent watertight when submerged, even on the most heavy-duty of off-road vehicles. Likewise, if you are wading in water that is deep enough to reach into the fresh air/heater system, you will find that water will seep in through the interior vents in the floor area and even through the dashboard! Therefore, to avoid shorting out the heater fan, never have your heater switched on when wading in really deep water. When you have finished, it may be worth switching the fan on to blow any remaining water out of the system.

As always, pick your route carefully, making sure that you can see the bottom. With the water as much as waist height, it is unlikely that you will want to walk out a route first, so instead drive through in first gear low, feeling the rocks and solidity of the riverbed through the vehicle's movements. If at any time you are unsure about the depth or feel as though the bed may be silty or muddy, don't take any chances – reverse back to a

shallower area and plan an alternative route. We recommend reversing back, as turning around in uncharted waters has its obvious dangers.

Finally, as an extra precaution, fit a tow rope to the front of the vehicle or rig your winch ready for use, just in case you require a tow out of trouble. If you have two ropes, fit one to the rear of the vehicle as well, as it may be impossible to get a tow forward once your vehicle has become stuck in the water. To save you getting unnecessarily wet if you do get stuck, the free end of the rope or winch should be placed on the bonnet or attached to your roof rack or roll cage (if fitted). Fitting a rope to the vehicle before entering the water also saves you from having to attach a rope blindly under the surface should you get stuck.

As a final word, can we reiterate that you

*Fig.99 Side slopes always feel worse from the driver's seat than they actually are, although you should always take care not to exceed the vehicle's maximum limit.*

should never attempt to ford water deeper than the top of the wheels without a snorkel fitted. Although the vehicle may be able to cope to a certain extent, there is very little margin for error should the level suddenly become deeper.

## SIDE SLOPES

Side slopes are possibly the most unnerving of all types of off-road obstacles, although it is safe to say that your nerve will probably have long gone before the vehicle actually topples over. Nevertheless it should be noted that the margin between an upright vehicle and a rolled one is wafer thin, so you should always be extremely wary of any sideways camber.

In general terms, the maximum side slope angle for a standard unladen vehicle is around 40 degrees, although there are many variables that will decrease this by a significant margin. Ground conditions are the first major factor to be looked at when considering a side slope. If you are on an extremely grippy surface (such as dry, solid rock), the diagonal angle of the side slope can be much greater than a slippery mud incline. With slippery ground conditions there is always the constant worry that the vehicle may slip sideways down the slope, thus causing enough momentum to tip the vehicle over. At all times take care!

Before attempting a side slope, look at the way that your vehicle is loaded. In general, heavy objects should be stored as low as possible in the vehicle, thus keeping the

*Fig.100 Take care when traversing side slopes if you have a heavily loaded roof rack.*

centre of gravity close to the ground. A roof rack fitted to your vehicle will significantly raise the vehicle's centre of gravity – even more so if it is heavily loaded. If you have to drive a side slope that looks as though it might be tricky, remove all heavy objects (such as a spare wheel, loaded jerry cans and a hi-lift jack) from the roof rack, only replacing them when you are back on level ground.

Before driving the side slope, get out and walk it to assess the best route and to look for any potential traps that might throw the vehicle off course, or – even worse – tip it over. Mounting a wheel over a large rock or into a hidden dip for example, may be enough to change the acceptable side slope angle, with possible disastrous consequences. If there are some ruts on the slope, use them to hold the vehicle on course; while the side of the lower rut can be used as a useful 'chock' to stop the vehicle slipping down the slope.

If there are no ruts and the ground is slippery, it is advisable to get your shovel out and dig some grooves to keep your vehicle from slipping down sideways. If a side slope feels particularly hazardous and you have a winch fitted to your vehicle, spool it out and anchor it to a sturdy tree or similar to act as an extra safety device. As you inch your way across the slope, spool it in so that it is constantly taut. Should the worst happen and the slope become too much for the vehicle, the tight winch rope should (in theory) keep you and your vehicle from rolling over.

If at any stage you start to feel the vehicle sliding sideways, or feel unsteady and think

*Fig.101 Side slopes with loose surfaces can be treacherous, as this Land Rover driver learnt!*

that it is about to roll over, quickly (but calmly) engage reverse gear low, feed on some lock and drive the vehicle down to the bottom of the hill in a controlled backwards descent. You can worry about getting the vehicle back onto the route when you have safely stopped at the bottom.

# DIFFERENT GROUND CONDITIONS: SAND AND SNOW

In the UK you are very unlikely to come across large areas of deep sand or snow, except on the beach or at certain times of the year. Although the techniques required for successful sand and snow driving will seldom be used by the majority of British off-roaders, they are worth knowing should you intend venturing further afield in your off-road adventures.

## Sand

Any off-roader who has driven on the soft sand of the desert will find it very hard to stifle a grin when reminiscing about their experiences. Put simply, sand driving is a lot of fun, and unless you do something really stupid, it is unlikely that either you or your vehicle will sustain any damage.

In the Middle East, 4x4 owners regularly take their vehicles wadi bashing, which is where each driver tries to get further up a sand dune than the others. Thanks to the power-sapping qualities of fine sand, a healthy dose of momentum is the only way to progress up the wadi, and in the case of some particularly steep dunes it is not unusual for vehicles to be doing in excess of 80mph as they start to climb.

As with all types of off-roading, on sand you should assess the route ahead of you to prepare yourself mentally for what lies

*Fig.102 Driving in soft sand can be a lot of fun.*

*Fig.103 Dropping your tyre pressures will help you keep moving.*

ahead. According to what you see, you may need to change to a higher or lower gear; you may need to increase your speed; or you may need to pick another route! Successful sand driving requires a little experience, and you will often find yourself getting stuck in the strangest of places.

When you sense that you are losing momentum, don't increase the power and spin the wheels in a vain attempt to get the vehicle moving again, as this will only dig your vehicle deeper into the sand making recovery difficult. Inevitably you will become stuck in sand, and the best way to recover a stuck vehicle in this situation is to jack it up and place sand ladders underneath the wheels to lift them back to the surface. Take care when feeding the sand ladders under the rotating wheels, and only apply the power gently to prevent digging yourself in further.

If you plan to do a lot of driving on sand, it is advisable to drop the tyre pressures of your vehicle to around 15psi to give a larger footprint, which will in turn help prevent the vehicle from digging a hole for itself. Similarly, your choice of tyre will help you keep moving on soft sand. Narrow mud tyres are definitely the wrong choice – fit instead the widest and smoothest tyre you can find. This will keep you on the surface rather than digging down under it.

Driving on hard compacted sand (such as that found on a beach near the water's edge) is much easier than driving on the soft stuff, although you should be aware that it could change to quicksand at any stage – in this case, there's no substitute for momentum. Nevertheless, you should try to avoid such areas at all costs, as recovering a stricken vehicle from quicksand is a laborious and labour-intensive procedure, and one that may require the services of a winch. If the tide is advancing rapidly, it can also be a relatively stressful operation!

## Snow

In the every once in a while that the UK is affected by a heavy snowfall, drivers of all 4x4 vehicles have a good reason to be smug. Having an extra pair of driven wheels means that all off-road vehicles have an instant advantage over two-wheel drives, which invariably suffer from a lack of traction on unsalted winter roads – remember that you don't have to be 'off-road' to encounter deep snow.

However, despite the fact that 4x4 vehicles have a distinct traction advantage in snowy conditions, it should be noted that just because your off-road vehicle is easy to drive on winter roads, you shouldn't make the all too common mistake of thinking that four-wheel drive gives you an advantage when it comes to braking. A four-wheel drive is just as susceptible to lock-ups and brake slides as a 'normal' car – you have been warned!

To a certain extent driving in snow is similar to off-roading in mud or sand, so the techniques required are more or less similar. Momentum is often the best way to get through, especially if the snow is quite fresh and no-one else has driven through it before. Relatively deep snowdrifts can often be crossed by charging through them, but before doing this it is vital to check that there is nothing underneath the drift that may cause damage to your vehicle. Whereas soft snow is unlikely to dent a vehicle's bodywork, a concealed rock most definitely will!

*Fig.104  Always use momentum to get through virgin snow, but make sure that there are no hidden dangers underneath the surface.*

*Fig.105 Be aware that a light sprinkling of snow can hide a layer of sheet ice.*

With all types of virgin snow it is vitally important to be constantly aware of what lies underneath the surface. Heavy snow can disguise large rocks, deep ditches and, perhaps the worst-case scenario, deep frozen water. At all times, try and follow the tracks of other vehicles in really snowy conditions; although there is a greater chance that you will become stuck, it is much better to be safe.

Going downhill in snow can occasionally be interesting, as the vehicle builds up momentum and starts to move quicker than the vehicle's engine braking. In this situation, braking gently may improve the situation, especially if this causes a slight build-up of snow in front of the wheels. However, if you find that this doesn't work, the last resort is steering off the track into some deeper snow that should hopefully halt your progress. Be aware that snow can hide patches of black ice – as always if ever in doubt, get out and check the route ahead on foot.

When going out in snowy conditions you should be prepared to get stuck. If you are travelling with another 4x4 then this shouldn't be too much of a problem, as the other vehicle will be able to offer a tow to get you moving again. If you are travelling by yourself, however, you should always carry a basic amount of survival gear just in case you have to spend time in the vehicle waiting for assistance. These items are just as applicable for winter on-road travel.

- Standard tow rope
- Flask with a hot drink
- Some energy-rich food
- A long-handled shovel
- A blanket and/or sleeping bag
- Some warm clothing and wellington boots.

Finally, if you live in an area that is susceptible to regular snowfall, you might like to
contemplate buying a set of snow chains. The
difference that snow chains make to traction
in snowy conditions is simply astounding;
especially when they are fitted to all four
wheels of an off-roader. If you only have one
pair of chains however, fit them to the front
wheels and benefit from improved traction
and steering.

# 6 Off-Road Recovery Techniques

It is an obvious but unwritten rule of off-roading that sooner or later you and your vehicle will become stuck! Whether that means that you cannot go any further forward without resorting to a winch or pull (up a steep slippery slope, for example), or – the more likely scenario – your vehicle is completely immobile, you will need to effect a recovery to get yourself moving again.

As discussed in the previous chapters, you should at all times read the ground ahead to anticipate whether or not you are likely

*Fig.106 The rope is the most important piece of recovery gear the off-roader should have, and it should always be in perfect condition.*

to become stuck, and if there is a high possibility that this will occur you should try to outline a mental strategy to effect the resulting recovery. As with all areas of off-roading, prior preparation – even if only for the short term – is an absolute must.

It is important that you realize precisely when you are stuck, as often – even if you have ceased forward motion – it is possible to reverse back out of the obstacle under your own power. If this isn't possible on the first or second attempt, don't try to extricate yourself *ad infinitum*, as you'll only make matters worse by digging yourself in. Instead, get out of the vehicle and assess the situation – why have you got stuck and what's the best way to get you unstuck ?

## OFF-ROAD RECOVERY EQUIPMENT

### Ropes

The rope is probably the most important piece of recovery equipment that the off-roader can have. Providing that you have some shackles and another (towing) vehicle that isn't stuck itself, the trusty rope will pull you out of most sticky situations.

It is important that the rope you have is man enough for the job. Most off-road vehicles weigh just under two tonnes when unladen and if you add the additional force required to pull a stuck vehicle free, the standard on-road tow rope sold in most garages is patently inadequate for the job – leave this for on-road towing. The ideal rope for the off-roader is a 24mm-diameter nylon weave that is rated up to twelve tonnes. Providing you don't try to recover a truck, this should be more than adequate for most off-road recoveries.

The length of an off-road tow rope is also an important consideration: generally speaking, long tow ropes are recommended

to keep the vehicles well apart. As well as ensuring that the towing vehicle doesn't have to get too close to the stricken vehicle (it, too, might become stuck), having a longer rope gives you a useful safety zone between the two vehicles should the stuck vehicle become unstuck more quickly than anticipated. The ideal length for an off-road recovery rope is around 4.5m or 15ft. It goes without saying that you should never use any type of rope that is damaged or frayed – when it breaks the consequences could be dire.

All nylon ropes have a certain amount of 'give' to prevent too much shock loading on vehicle recovery points, and this stretching action can be beneficial to the recovery process. By building up and then releasing stored kinetic energy, the specially woven KERR (Kinetic Energy Recovery Rope) is a remarkably effective recovery tool, providing a gentle but strong pull that will recover all but the most severely stuck vehicles.

To get the best pulling power from a KERR there is a specific procedure that must be followed, and we shall look at this later in this chapter.

### Shackles

Assuming that your rope has been properly spliced with a hoop at either end, you will need to use a shackle to attach it to your vehicle's recovery point. Shackles come in many different shapes and sizes, and you should never be tempted to use a shackle that is too small or inadequate for the load being placed upon it.

As well as the various different size shackles that are available, there are also two types: the rounded bow shackle and the straighter 'D' shackle. For off-road use the bow shackle is probably the more useful of the two, as its increased internal diameter gives plenty of space to fit thick ropes, hooks or a snatch block for winching.

When assembling a shackle you should always put the screw-in crossbar on the side nearest the vehicle and remember not to over-tighten it. Once you have screwed in the crossbar as far as it will go, unscrew it by a half turn to prevent it from jamming as load is put upon the shackle. This is particularly important, as a stuck shackle is very difficult to unscrew.

## The Hi-Lift Jack

It has been suggested that you can go anywhere in the world with a 4x4, a tow rope, some shackles and a hi-lift jack, and thanks to the hi-lift's variety of uses this statement is not far from the truth. The basic design of the hi-lift is rumoured to have been around since the beginning of the twentieth century, where it was first seen in the farmyard as a general purpose tool with a number of uses. Nowadays the hi-lift tends to be used more as an off-road recovery tool than a farmyard all-rounder, although there are a number of non-off-roading applications to which the hi-lift can be put to.

The actual jack itself consists of two main components: the mechanical jack head and the rack on which it fits, which can vary from four to five feet in length. Using two pins that spring in and out of a series of holes in the rack, the head can be moved up or down the rack by the movement of the jack handle. The direction of travel is selected by moving a side-mounted lever up or down as appropriate, and to be safe you should always ensure that this lever is in the upright position when there is a load on the jack. Similarly, the jack handle should always be returned to the upright position when not in use, to prevent it from being knocked and flying dangerously out of control with a load on the jack.

*Fig.107 Always ensure that the direction lever on a hi-lift jack is in the upright position when there is a load on the jack.*

The lifting ratio of a hi-lift is approximately 30:1, so lifting the front end of the average off-roader doesn't require a herculean amount of effort. You will note also that the hi-lift has a relatively large base to keep it upright, as well as a protruding piece on the jack head that can be placed under anything flat to be lifted.

Although this piece on the jack head can be used directly under Land Rover bumpers and rear crossmembers, for most winch bumpers you can fit a special accessory that offers a lot more security when jacking. As this piece slots over the base of the jack head and fits in a hole in the winch bumper, there

*Fig.108 Using an extra 'foot' to spread the load will prevent the jack from sinking in really muddy conditions.*

is no possibility of the jack becoming dislodged or knocked out from under the vehicle – a very worthwhile safety device. Another useful accessory to have with your hi-lift is a larger jack pad which prevents the base from sinking deep into the mud, thanks to the larger footprint created by the additional pad.

Before leaving the hi-lift for now, it should be repeated that, although the hi-lift is an extremely useful tool, it is absolutely imperative that you use it properly to avoid injury. Above all, remember to: i) return the jack handle to the upright position when not in use, and ii) always make sure that the jack reversing lever is in the 'up' position when-

ever there is a load on the jack. The exception to this, of course, is when you wish to lower the load back down under control.

## The Airbag Jack

The airbag jack wasn't originally designed for use off-road – instead it was developed for emergency recovery of overturned tankers and aeroplanes, when a gentle low-pressure lift is imperative to cause minimum damage and extra caution must be taken not to risk igniting the inflammable liquid carried within. Of course, these airbags are much larger than the type used for off-road recoveries but their operation remains the same. The military also use airbags to recover tanks and heavy trucks off-road, so their credentials are sound.

Whereas the larger recovery airbag jacks use compressors for inflation, off-road airbags make use of the exhaust gases emitted by your engine, and there is a long nozzled pipe supplied with the kit to bring the gases to the bag. It is imperative to keep this pipe kink-free to ensure a quick and smooth inflation – if you don't then the airbag will simply not work and you will have a hard job keeping the nozzle on the exhaust. The back pressure might also stall the engine if you're not careful.

Airbag jacks are particularly useful for vehicles that do not have hi-lift jacking points, which apart from Land Rover Defenders and other 'workhorse' type 4x4s means the majority of off-road vehicles. You can fit bumper bars or sill protectors for use with a hi-lift jack (see Chapter 3), but using an airbag is a more straightforward solution.

As a result, the uses for an airbag jack off-road are similar to those of a hi-lift – that is to say, for lifting a vehicle clear of ruts and slewing it to one side, for changing a wheel in off-road conditions, or for lifting the wheels clear of the ground so that rocks, and so on,

*Fig.109 An airbag jack can be used to lift a vehicle clear of ruts.*

can be placed underneath for improved traction. The airbag jack is also useful for recoveries in boggy areas, where its low ground pressure and large 'footprint' is a definite bonus. Like the hi-lift, the airbag jack can be a little unstable at full extension, so you must take care when using it.

Care must also be taken with the positioning of the airbag jack. Like the hi-lift, you can't just jack off any part of the body, as doing so will probably damage the vehicle as excessive stress is placed on body components. Instead, try to use areas near the chassis, or strong structural components such as sills or bumpers. Be careful not to place the jack near the hot exhaust system though, as you risk damaging both the jack and the exhaust.

Before inflating the jack, check that the top is parallel to the area being jacked onto and that the base is as far under the vehicle as possible. The airbag doesn't always inflate uniformly, and you risk having the jack in a very unstable position if the top and bottom are out of line. A rubber mat placed on top of the jack will help the top 'grip' the body component, but if you still have problems, stop inflation by simply pulling off the nozzle from the end of the exhaust – take care not to become covered in soot at this point, however!

A non-return valve in the bag connector holds the exhaust gases in the bag, so you must make sure that this is correctly inserted and that there is no leakage. When you want to deflate the bag, simply pull out this connector and let the pressure expel the exhaust gases. To completely deflate it, you will probably have to kneel on top of the bag to get them all out. Beware of course, of the dangers of breathing in toxic exhaust gases.

115

## The Tirfor Hand Winch

The Tirfor hand winch is a relatively cheap alternative to a vehicle-mounted electric winch, and well worth carrying in the vehicle for self-recovery purposes. Although it requires a lot more effort to use than an electric winch, the Tirfor is a lot more flexible when it comes to off-road recoveries. An electric winch could let you down (through a dead engine, flat battery, lack of maintenance or a broken cable) and problems are often encountered when a front-mounted electric winch is facing the wrong way for the best recovery angle. The Tirfor is much more versatile as you can use it to winch a vehicle from any angle, although using it for long periods of time is hard work. As with most winch recoveries, you should have the wheels spinning in first gear low on tickover to assist the winch.

In normal use off-road (in an assisted recovery), a Tirfor should manage to move the vehicle about three metres per minute. The maximum lifting load for a mid-range Tirfor is around 2.5 tonnes, so it should be more than adequate for recovering all types of 4x4 (with the obvious exception of large off-road trucks). If the vehicle is very heavily bogged (that is, if the axles are buried in deep), use a hi-lift jack to raise the vehicle clear of the suction effect of the ground, and then place some small rocks underneath the raised wheels, taking care that the vehicle is stable on the jack and that the rocks will not damage the vehicle underneath once it is lowered onto them. With a manual winch, any reduction on effort will be extremely worthwhile!

Use of the Tirfor hand winch is extremely straightforward, however it is beyond the brief of this book to go into a blow by blow account of exactly how to use it – instead consult the owner's manual that comes with the winch. The device's mechanism feeds a special wire rope through two sets of jaws

*Fig.110 The tirfor hand winch is a useful tool to have for self-recovery.*

that, inch by inch, feed the rope from one to the other thus pulling the wire through. The Tirfor itself needs to be anchored to a solid object (a tree or parked vehicle) to prevent it being pulled forward towards the stuck vehicle. Use a strop or shackle to do this, connecting it to the hook that is positioned at one end of the winch.

Once the stuck vehicle is recovered, release the tension on the rope and pull the wire through. Take extra care when winching through wet mud that the cable does not become too muddy, as the relatively intricate internal workings of the unit may become damaged or worn with the abrasive action of the mud. Likewise, take extra care of the wire cable, as a damaged or kinked cable will have difficulty passing through the sets of jaws within the unit. As with all types of winching, wear gloves at all times to prevent your hands becoming cut with burrs on the wire rope.

## TYPES OF RECOVERY

### Self-Recovery

If you are off-roading in a single vehicle (remember, this is not recommended) and get stuck, then you have no option but to get yourself going again on your own. As we discussed earlier, as soon as you are stuck you must assess the situation to find out what exactly is preventing you from carrying on. Without meaning to state the obvious, becoming stuck means that your wheels have insufficient grip to overcome the load or resistance being imposed on the vehicle. To get yourself unstuck, you will have to overcome this lack of grip or provide an alternative means of moving the vehicle.

Let's say for example that your vehicle has become high centred in deep ruts. To overcome the lack of forward motion in this situation, you need to raise the level of the ground underneath the wheels to re-establish traction and get you going again. By far the best way of doing this is by placing

*Fig.111 With the right number of people available to lend a hand, self-recovery is relatively straightforward!*

*Fig.112 Hooking up to another vehicle is one of the easiest types of recovery. You must always ensure that your ropes and recovery points can take the load, however.*

solid objects under the wheels, such as large rocks or fallen branches. This should be done with extreme care, however, and you should be aware of not destroying the countryside around you in search of appropriate items to place underneath the wheels.

If you are unable to get the vehicle moving again using methods such as this, then the only other option for self-recovery is the use of a winch, tirfor or hi-lift jack to physically move the vehicle out of trouble. We shall cover this type of recovery in a later section.

## Towing/Snatch Recovery

For all intents and purposes, hooking up a rope to another vehicle and getting a tow out of trouble is by far the quickest and simplest means to get yourself unstuck. However, this relies very much on there being a second vehicle available to be used as a tug, and also assumes that it is possible for it to get close enough to the stuck vehicle without this second vehicle becoming bogged down itself. Occasionally it is possible to attach a number of ropes together to create a long rope, but if the stuck vehicle is really a long way from *terra firma*, then care must be taken not to end up with two stricken vehicles.

There are two types of tow recovery: the straight pull with a piece of dead rope, and the snatch recovery that makes use of the ingenious Kinetic Energy Recovery Rope which offers a significant increase in the tow vehicle's potential pulling power. The straight pull with the dead rope requires the rope to be pulled taut, and only after this has been done can the towing vehicle apply the power. For most recovery situations this is perfectly adequate, but for really stuck vehicles the KERR recovery is the best option.

At this stage it is worth noting that all types of tow recovery are potentially dangerous, yet none more so than a high force 'snatch' type recovery. Just consider for a moment the forces that are at play and you will see what I mean. It is therefore very important to take a good look at the recovery points available on the vehicle before you tow (or winch) a vehicle out of a stuck position. The vehicle preparation discussed in Chapter 3 should have made you

realize just how important strong recovery points are for safe and effective rescue.

At no stage should you attempt to use the manufacturer's lashing eyes that have been put there to hold the vehicle in place while on a car transporter. The stresses of a heavy pull would at the very least bend these inwards, but in addition to this you also risk the possibility of them breaking, which could result in serious injury or damage to your vehicle. In short, always ensure that recovery points are 'man' enough to take the strain.

The best recovery points are made from galvanized steel and are directly bolted to the chassis using high-tensile steel bolts. Never attach any type of rope to a point out of line with the chassis (the top of a bull bar for example), and beware of rusty areas that

*Fig.113 Beware of bringing your tow vehicle too close to the vehicle that is stuck; the last thing you want is for the tow vehicle to become stuck as well!*

could prove to be a weak link. One well-known case among off-road circles is a military-specification NATO hitch that came away from a rusty rear crossmember on an aging Land Rover during a snatch recovery. Once detached from the vehicle it rocketed forwards on the rope, smashing through the towing vehicle's rear window and out through the front windscreen. It was only luck that saved the driver from being seriously injured or even killed as the heavy NATO hitch flew through the vehicle, missing him by inches.

The next possible weak link in the recovery chain is the rope itself. Any rope that has become frayed or damaged should be cut up and discarded immediately, as a snapping rope is a potential death trap when placed under heavy load. We recommend using either a 4.5m x 24mm nylon 'dead' rope, or an 8m x 24mm Kinetic Energy Recovery Rope. Both of these are rated at twelve tons safe load, so it is unlikely that they will break unless frayed or well used.

Providing that you are satisfied with the recovery points and rope, then the next step is to plan the way that you intend to pull the vehicle out of trouble. This normally depends on the safe location of the towing vehicle, which could be as far as five metres away. The last thing you want to do is bring the tow vehicle in too close and get it stuck as well!

If the vehicle being recovered is stuck particularly badly, you will want to exert the maximum amount of pull possible from both vehicles, and to do so you will need to have both vehicles driving. In order to synchronize the proceedings, you can use a short hoot on the horn to signal that both parties are ready for the recovery or, better still, a CB radio fitted to both vehicles will allow the drivers to talk to one another as the recovery takes place. This way, once the vehicle is clear of the obstacle, the driver of the vehicle being recovered can pass the message on to the tow vehicle very easily.

## KERR Recovery

As discussed above, the Kinetic Energy Recovery Rope (KERR) recovery is much more controlled than a straightforward pull, yet because high forces are at work within the recovery, you should be extra cautious of the dangers of frayed ropes and defective recovery points

The KERR recovery operates on the 'elastic band' principle to extract vehicles from the mud, with the rope storing kinetic energy to help give extra force to extract a stricken vehicle. It works like this: as the tow vehicle drives away at a reasonably brisk pace, the elastic KERR rope becomes tighter and begins to stretch. Once it has reached its limit the taut rope then begins to pull out the stuck vehicle, but as it begins to move the rope tries to contract back to its normal pre-stretched size. As it does so, a little extra energy is applied to pull out the stuck vehicle, thus the KERR offers a greater force of pull than standard 'dead' ropes.

As well as this increased force, another benefit of the stretchy kinetic rope is its smooth operation when compared to conventional 'dead' ropes. Because the KERR stretches and then compresses back like a spring, the sudden jolt associated with dead rope recoveries is eliminated. Instead, being recovered by a KERR is somewhat akin to a huge helping hand coming behind and pushing the vehicle out of trouble – a much safer and more comfortable way to be recovered.

To get the best performance from a KERR there is a basic operating procedure that should be followed for every recovery. Although you can just hook up the rope to both vehicles and drive on, if you want to get the maximum pulling force from the kinetic rope it pays to use the correct method of operation.

Assuming that you have checked that both vehicles' recovery points are strong enough

*Fig.114   Use a bridle to centre the tow directly in front of the vehicle.*

*Fig.115  It is very important that you lay out the kinetic energy rope in the correct way.*

121

to take the pull, bring the tow vehicle back to about two metres in front of the vehicle to be recovered and attach the rope to the rear recovery point. Next, lay the KERR out between the two vehicles in a recurring snake-like 'S' pattern and attach it to the front of the vehicle to be recovered using a bridle.

The bridle allows you to ensure that the towing force is concentrated along the centre line of the vehicle rather than off to one side. To use a bridle however, you will need to ensure that the vehicle being rescued has two front-mounted recovery points or that the spring hangers on the front of the chassis are up to the job. If not, then attaching the KERR to a side recovery point is acceptable but not ideal.

With this set-up in place, the drivers should be ready in both vehicles, preferably with a CB radio each for communication. The tow vehicle should set off at a relatively brisk pace, applying the power smoothly and being prepared to keep it on as the rope becomes taut. In most circumstances the KERR will allow you to recover the stricken vehicle on the first attempt, but if not, reverse the towing vehicle back and set up the rope again for another go. If you cannot get the vehicle out after three attempts it is well and truly stuck and you will need to consider another means of recovery – probably using a winch and a bit of digging.

## THE MANY USES OF A HI-LIFT JACK

As explained earlier, the hi-lift jack isn't suitable for every type of 4x4 on the market, but with a little modification it can be used with the majority of vehicles. With a little ingenuity, the hi-lift can be useful in all types of off-road situation. From lifting a vehicle out of deep ruts to being used as a type of hand winch, the hi-lift is an extremely capable

tool: we've even seen one being used as an emergency support for an engine after an engine mount failed, although this use isn't mentioned in the manual!

To use the hi-lift with most off-road vehicles a special adapter tool is recommended, and this fits in most types of winch bumper and 'roo bar'. If you don't have one of these, however, a yellow jate ring attached to a NATO hitch or Bushey Hall recovery point can be used as an alternative. As always, care must be taken when jacking as the hi-lift is potentially very unstable. To prevent the jack from falling over (especially necessary as the jack head is further up the rack), place a steadying hand on the top of the rack, leaving the other to operate the jack handle. As mentioned earlier, ensure that the handle is placed in the upright position when you are not jacking – any other position is simply unsafe.

## Lifting the Vehicle Clear of Ruts

For our first example of the hi-lift jack's usefulness let's imagine that your vehicle has become high-centred in some deep ruts. Any type of forward progress is very difficult as the underside of the vehicle is dragging on some very dense mud – the best way to carry on would be to raise the vehicle by a few inches. Enter the hi-lift jack!

By raising the front wheels out of the ruts using the jack, you and your co-driver can place rocks, branches or logs under the wheels to give some much-needed lift. Once you've added enough to raise the underside clear of the rut centres, lower the vehicle onto the rocks/logs and with a gentle application of power you should be able to drive on.

Note that you should never put any part of your body underneath a vehicle supported by a hi-lift jack, and that any rocks or branches that you collect to fill in the ruts should be removed with absolute concern for the environment. This technique is equally applicable for vehicles stuck in fine sand, although sand ladders should be used in place of rocks and branches.

## Breaking the Suction in a Bog

Another common use for the hi-lift jack is breaking the suction when stuck firmly in a bog. Like the example cited above, in excessively boggy conditions the vehicle's chassis and axles cause a tremendous amount of drag when the vehicle has sunk down low. In this case a straight tow or winch is unable to extract the vehicle without a little extra assistance.

Using the hi-lift, jack the front of the vehicle up in the air. This may be a little difficult at first, as the vehicle will be very heavy thanks to the suction effect of the bog. You may need to use a sand ladder underneath the jack foot to help spread out the weight – without this in extremely boggy conditions the jack will tend to sink and the vehicle will go nowhere!

With the front wheels raised clear of the bog, place some sand ladders underneath and lower the vehicle back down. With care, the vehicle can now be driven or winched forward, although once again care must be taken not to overdo it. Spinning the wheels excessively will dig the vehicle back down into the bog and you will be back to where you started.

*Fig.116 Using a hi-lift jack to break the suction of a bog under a vehicle will greatly assist your winch.*

## Lifting and Slewing

As mentioned above, the hi-lift jack is a relatively unstable unit. Although this isn't normally a problem, this instability can actually be used to your advantage when off-roading. Let's imagine that you are high-centred in ruts again, but this time it is impossible to continue forward as the ruts are just too deep. To keep going on this track, the only choice would be to straddle the ruts by placing one wheel either side – but how to get the vehicle up above the surface of the ruts?

As we mentioned earlier, once your wheels are in ruts it is almost impossible to drive out of them, so the only means of getting the vehicle out of the ruts is to use the lifting and slewing technique with the hi-lift jack. After positioning the jack at the centre of the front bumper, jack the vehicle up so that the front wheels are around six inches above the top of the ruts. As the jack head climbs higher up the rack you will note that the whole combination becomes very unstable, so it is imperative that you have two helpers positioned at either side of the vehicle to prevent it from sliding over prematurely.

With the vehicle lifted well clear of the ruts get your helpers to move well out of the way, and taking a lot of care yourself, push the jack to one side. Providing that the front wheels have been lifted up high enough, the wheels should fall outside the ruts and the front of the vehicle is clear. You can now assess whether it will be possible to continue with the rear wheels still in the ruts. If not, simply repeat the process for the back wheels, thus positioning both front and rear wheels completely out of the ruts.

*Fig.117 Demonstrating the lifting and slewing technique with a hi-lift jack. Before toppling the vehicle over to one side, make sure that your volunteers are well clear of it.*

## Using the Hi-Lift as a Winch

Although obviously not designed as such, the hi-lift jack can serve as a useful hand winch for emergency use. Firstly find an appropriate anchor, and using some chain connect the top of the hi-lift rack to it (remember to use a strop first if your anchor is a tree). Next, position the jack head at the bottom of the rack and connect another chain from it to the stuck vehicle. Tighten both chains so that there is no slack and start to lever the lifting mechanism up the rack – the vehicle should now start to move forward.

If you have reached the top of the rack and the vehicle is still unable to move under its own steam, you will need to lash the vehicle off and start all over again. Using a rope, connect your vehicle to the anchor ensuring that the rope is tight enough not to allow any

movement backwards – the last thing you want is to undo all your hard work with the hi-lift! Guide the jack head back to the bottom of the hi-lift rack and reconnect the vehicle to the anchor using the chains as described above. You are now ready to start again.

## WINCHING

As we discussed in Chapter 3, a front-mounted electric winch is a useful lifeline for the off-roader – especially one who tends to go off-roading solo. Without any additional vehicles to offer a tow, a winch (either manual or electric) is the only way you will be able to extract your vehicle from the mire. As such, the winch's usefulness should not be underestimated. Having one bolted to the

*Fig.118 Although it is hard work to operate, you can use a hi-lift as a hand winch.*

*Fig.119 A front-mounted winch is an extremely useful tool for the serious off-roader, although its use in recreational off-road is fairly recent.*

front of your vehicle instantly expands the type of terrain you and your vehicle can explore, although it is very important to know how to use it properly. Remember that winching is dangerous and safety should always be top priority.

## Winching Safely

Any type of recovery places enormous stresses on the vehicle's recovery points and rope, and winching is no exception. In a sense, winching is more dangerous than conventional tow recoveries as the wire winch rope can cause a lot more damage should it snap under load. If you follow these simple do's and don'ts when winching, then you should have no problems at all.

Every winch and its wire rope has been thoroughly tested by the manufacturer, and there is a sizable inbuilt safety margin to give extra piece of mind. Nevertheless, any weak links (such as a frayed rope or poorly secured hook) will negate this margin, possibly resulting in serious injury or even death. Winching is a serious matter, so you should never take any risks or shortcuts. Below is a list of winching do's and don'ts:

- Don't ever use a winch cable that is frayed or damaged.
- Do ensure that there are at least four complete turns on the winch drum before winching. Never winch with the wire rope fully extended.
- Don't ever cross a winch cable when it is under load or taut.

*Fig.120 Always use sturdy winching gloves when operating or handling the winch.*

- Do keep well away from the cable at all times.
- Do make sure that the vehicle's recovery points are up to the job. Never use lashing eyes for winching or any type of recovery.
- Don't handle a winch cable without wearing proper winching gloves.
- Don't put any part of your body (including loose clothing) near a turning winch drum.
- Don't let the cable slide through your hands when it is going in. Instead use a hand-over-hand movement to guide it in. Never attempt to feed a cable onto the drum when it is under load.

If you follow these simple rules when winching, then extracting your vehicle should be a relatively safe operation.

Remember that there are no shortcuts when winching, and that you should never be in a hurry to get the vehicle out – take your time and remain safe.

## Winch Accessories

Every winch owner must have a comprehensive range of accessories for safe and easy operation of his/her winch in an off-road environment. Like all types of off-road equipment, there are several 'must haves' that are vital for safe and convenient use of the winch, while certain other accessories are not vital, but are extremely useful for many types of off-road recovery.

Perhaps the most important winching accessory is a stout pair of winching gloves.

These should be gloves specifically designed for winching, as these are normally made of heavy-duty canvas type material or even leather. Winching gloves are generally loose fitting around the wrist and should pull off relatively easily. This is to prevent your hand from being dragged into a moving drum should the glove become snagged on the winch cable – instead the glove should slip off and enter harmlessly into the wire, leaving your hand intact. In short, don't use gardening gloves as these are likely to fray or wear easily and often feature elasticated wrists.

When winching you will always need to use something as an anchor, the most common being another vehicle or a tree. With a second vehicle all you have to do is connect the winch hook to a shackle on the vehicle's recovery point, but when winching

off a tree you have be a lot more sympathetic – you should never wrap the wire rope around the tree for example, as the damage caused is almost certain to kill it.

Instead, a heavy-duty webbing tree strop should be looped around the tree trunk, as this allows you to successfully winch off the tree without any fear of damage. You should always place the tree strop as low down the trunk as possible, and the eyes at the end should be connected together using a bow shackle on which you can hook the winch rope. Like winch wires and off-road recovery ropes, never use a tree strop that is cut or frayed. The possibility of damage or injury if it breaks is just too great.

For most winch recoveries the standard 30m (100ft) wire rope is more than sufficient, but for recoveries that require a little more length, an extension wire rope can be fitted

*Fig.121 Always use a tree strop to winch off trees. Make sure that it is placed down as low as possible.*

to double the reach. Like the original wire rope itself, the extension wire should be of the same diameter and in perfect condition. To keep your extension wire rope in top-notch condition, you might like to consider storing it inside an old bike tyre to keep it safe.

One of the most useful (and perhaps under-rated) accessories that a winch-equipped vehicle can have is a snatch block. Not to be confused with a snatch recovery, the snatch block is a basic pulley that features two swingaway supports that can be locked by a shackle, and it has a number of uses. If all winch pulls were in a straight line or if the pull required never exceeded 1,000lb, then all winching jobs would be easy. Unfortunately this is seldom the case but the snatch block can be used to assist.

Firstly the snatch block can be used to change the direction of pull – something that is useful for ensuring that the wire is pulling directly ahead of the vehicle or to ensure that the sturdiest anchor is being used. Secondly the pulley effect of a snatch block can reduce the load on the winch by using basic physics to increase the mechanical advantage of the winch. We shall look at this further when we discuss the various uses of a snatch block later on in this chapter.

When using a snatch block to straighten an angled pull, you should attach the snatch block to a sturdy anchor that is approximately 90 degrees to the front of the vehicle. You can do this by running a rope from this anchor to the snatch block that should be positioned directly in front of the vehicle. Be sure that the snatch block is sufficiently far enough in front of the vehicle to allow for a good pull – there's little point in positioning it a couple of metres ahead when you need to winch for at least four. As always with any type of recovery, make sure that the secondary anchor is strong enough to take the forces involved, and that the rope used to attach the snatch block is in a good state.

*Fig.122 Use a snatch block to alter the direction of pull.*

## Winching Procedure

The first question to ask yourself when rigging up a winch is: 'What should I anchor it to?' Obviously the answer to this will depend very much on the situation that you are in, but the necessity to anchor the winch to something secure is obvious.

In an ideal situation there would always be another vehicle or tree directly ahead of the vehicle, but as this is seldom the case the best way to find your anchor is to stand directly in front of your vehicle and look for the sturdiest tree in sight. Although an anchor

*Fig.123 The winch operator should always be in command of the situation. Make sure that they stand well clear of the rotating drum.*

that is directly in front of the vehicle is useful, do not be tempted to use a small tree that is straight ahead when there is a much sturdier one a few feet to one side. If you are using another vehicle to winch off, make sure that someone is inside it to operate the brakes, and chocking the vehicle or attaching it to something solid is also advisable.

When using a tree as an anchor, always use a tree strop to avoid damaging the sensitive bark. Place the tree strop as low as you can around the trunk, and if your strop is long enough wrap it twice around the tree to prevent it from moving when the winch is operating. Never winch off trees that look as though they will not be able to cope with the

load of the vehicle, and pay close attention to dead trees or stumps that you are using. If at any time they start to become uprooted, stop winching immediately and look for another anchor.

Once you have decided what you are going to winch off, pull out the cable from the drum using the winch's freespool setting. This allows you to walk out at your own pace, pulling out the correct amount of cable. One handy tip when pulling the cable out is to remember to take the tree strop and shackle with you at the same time. Doing so prevents you from having to make a second journey back to the vehicle to collect the vital accessories that you forgot the first time!

The next thing to consider is whether to

use a straight line pull or to double the cable up using a snatch block. For vehicles that are only slightly bogged a straight line pull will be sufficient, but for vehicles that are really stuck the mechanical advantage of a snatch block will help reduce the stress on the winch. Remember also that the less cable on the drum, the more powerful the pull. Just as the fitment of larger wheels and tyres will increase the gearing of a vehicle, the build-up of layers of wire rope on the winch drum effectively increases its diameter and gearing. In this case, having plenty of cable out will increase the pulling power of the

*Fig.124 Using a snatch block will greatly increase the pulling power of the winch.*

winch, but you should never have less than four wraps of cable on the drum. Any less and you risk pulling the wire off the drum!

The next question you have to ask is: 'Who will be the winch operator?' With the remote control it is perfectly feasible to operate the winch from the driver's seat, but there should also be someone outside the vehicle to oversee the wire going back on the drum. If you are controlling the winch from inside the cab, it is worth wrapping the remote control wire around the wing mirror to prevent any slack from falling off the bonnet and becoming caught under the wheels.

Assuming that there is someone else to watch the cable onto the drum, that person should be responsible for the safe operation of the winch. They should tell the person with the remote control when to winch in, winch out and stop. Although it is possible to transmit these instructions verbally, it is preferable to use the internationally agreed winch signals to prevent any confusion. A rotating hand raised above the head signals the operator to winch in; a rotating hand below the head means winch out. A raised palm means stop, while two palms signifies an emergency stop. To prevent any confusion there should only be one person responsible for these signs, and their authority is absolute.

As you would do when driving normally, you should always plan your route ahead when winching. Check the track for tree roots and hidden rocks that would increase the load on the winch as they go under the vehicle. Likewise, you should always ensure that the vehicle isn't hung up on a root or rock in the first place – it could be that the simple removal of this will free the vehicle without winching.

As the winch wire begins to wrap itself around the drum, try to feed it onto the drum evenly. This will prevent the cable from becoming damaged and will reduce the amount of 'natural' power loss. If at any time during the pull the cable starts to bunch, stop winching, unreel the cable and start again after you have respooled it on evenly. If you don't, then you risk damaging your winch cable unnecessarily. Remember that a damaged winch cable should always be replaced to maintain your safety margin.

There is much debate in off-roading circles as to whether you should supply drive to the wheels or not while winching. Doing so can assist the winch during particularly arduous pulls, but should you suddenly get traction then you risk 'overtaking' the winch and causing damage to the cable. Either way, it is very important to keep the engine running when winching to supply power to the battery, which will be working hard supplying current to the hard-working winch

motor. For an optimum charge, keep the revs at around 2,000 rpm.

If you do decide to winch in with the vehicle's wheels turning, be very careful of overrunning the winch as this will cause the cable to run loose on the drum, and possibly damage it. Sudden traction creates slack in the winch rope, only for the vehicle's weight to then snatch back upon the rope when grip is lost. By far the best solution is to spin the wheels slowly on tickover, or match the amount of drive according to the ground conditions ahead. If the ground conditions are very slippy with little chance of grip, then spin away. However, if there is a chance that traction will be gained, proceed with caution ready to cut the power to the wheels. Alternatively just stop winching if complete

*Fig.125 Make sure that your ground anchors stay in place while you are winching.*

traction is available, although make sure that someone is ready to pull the cable up out of the way of the wheels – using gloves of course.

## Ground Anchors

By far the best anchors for winching are another vehicle or a stout tree, but occasionally you may have access to neither in which case you will have to 'make' your own. As we discussed in Chapter 3, there are a number of different ground anchors available, but their ultimate purpose remains the same: to provide sufficient hold to pull the vehicle out of trouble.

Therefore, when using ground anchors it is extremely important to make sure that they stay in place while winching. Unlike trees, you can position your ground anchors anywhere, so it stands to reason that they should always be positioned in a straight line in front of the vehicle. Always make sure that the anchor is far enough ahead of the vehicle to allow it to winch itself clear of the obstacle, and ensure that the ground is firm enough to take the load. If at any stage the ground anchor starts to lift itself out of the ground, stop winching and find an alternative spot to place the anchors. As always, safety when winching is paramount.

# 7 Where to Go Off-Road – at Home and Abroad

## THE LEGAL SITUATION OF OFF-ROADING IN THE UK

Before setting out to drive off-road you should know where you are going. Although it may sound obvious, you cannot just pull off the tarmac and drive off on the first muddy field that you come across. Every acre of ground in the UK belongs to somebody, and driving along a track on which you have no right to drive will leave you open to charges of trespass.

Broadly speaking, in England the legal rights of way on which you can drive a wheeled vehicle can be divided into three categories: RUPPs, BOATs and UCRs. RUPP stands for Road Used as a Public Path; BOAT, Byway Open to All Traffic and UCR, Unclassified County Road.

In the 1960s the national Ordnance Survey maps simply showed all rights of way as white roads, but the government of the time requested the local county and parish councils to classify their tracks as public footpaths, bridleways, RUPPs or BOATs. Footpaths, bridleways and BOATs were relatively easy to classify, but there was some confusion as to the exact definition of a RUPP. As such, some RUPPs can never be driven by a 4x4 vehicle, being too narrow, too dangerous or too boggy.

To overcome this, all county councils have been requested by law to reclassify their RUPPs as BOATs, bridleways or footpaths, thus ending any possible confusion. Due to the potential for misinterpretation

Fig.126 *Always make sure that you know where you are going before setting off.*

and the serious possibility of losing a lane due to certain individuals' opposition to off-roading, this procedure is likely to take a long time. Some councils have finished their classification while others have a long way to go. Writing in 1997, RUPPs are still very much in evidence, but there will be a time when the only tracks that can be driven by the off-roader will be BOATs and UCRs.

In Scotland the situation is rather different. Due to the application of Scottish Law, there are only two rights of way in Scotland that you can drive without express permission. Obviously there are a large number of other tracks that are suitable for off-roading, but in every case you will have to get written permission from the landowner in order to drive them. As a result, if you want to go off-roading in Scotland, the best solution is to get in touch with one of the local off-road clubs or a Scottish off-road school to see when they are next planning to make a trip.

## HOW TO GO ABOUT RESEARCHING ROUTES

Due to the complex legal situation of public off-roading in the UK, one of the best bits of advice we can give is to join a local club which will have a rights of way officer who will point you in the right direction as far as local green lanes are concerned. You simply cannot just go and drive anywhere you like, so it is extremely important that you know that you have a right to be where you are driving.

*Fig.127 When off-roading in the UK it is imperative that you stick to legal rights of way.*

*Fig.128 Discovering Britain by 4x4 is very enjoyable, especially if you have researched the routes yourself.*

For many people the act of researching routes themselves is part of the off-road experience, and the process of doing this is relatively straightforward. Firstly you will need to buy the relevant Ordnance Survey 'Landranger' map for the area you are interested in and, using a magnifying glass, examine the map to find the relevant RUPPs and BOATs which are identifiable as a series of red dot/dash/dot and dot/cross/dot lines respectively. You should always ensure that the map you have is the latest version as rights of way are constantly being reclassified. Note however, that the existence of a BOAT or RUPP on the map doesn't necessarily make it a legal right of way – byways are regularly down or upgraded by the local council.

You might also like to look at minor roads on the map (shown as a series of parallel unbroken or broken black lines), which will more often than not be a UCR or Unclassified County Road. Although some of these will be tarmacked and of little interest to the off-roader, many UCRs offer some interesting and scenic terrain that can often only be driven by a four-wheel drive vehicle. Note once again that the existence of a UCR on a Landranger map doesn't necessarily make it a legal right of way. But how do you know which tracks are rights of way if the Ordnance Survey map cannot supply this information ?

The only place to discover the legal rights of way is on the 'definitive map' held at the Rights of Way Office at County Hall. The definitive map is a regularly updated large-scale map showing all the local public footpaths, bridleways, RUPPs and BOATs. Using this, you should check your maps to ensure that all the routes you would like to drive are indeed legal rights of way and are not subject to any TROs (Traffic Regulation Order) or reclassifications. If you have any doubts about the legality of tracks, strike them from your map. If you drive a legally closed track not only are you trespassing, you are also tarnishing the public image of off-roading.

For UCRs, you will need to visit the Highways Office at County Hall (this may be in the same office as the Rights of Way department), where you can consult the 'spider maps' showing the priority of maintenance. 'Unmetalled minor roads' are the ones of interest to off-roaders, and these should be relatively well marked. Nevertheless, it should be noted that even though a UCR is marked on the map, this is no guarantee of its drivability. Some UCRs are almost impossible to drive, so if you find a route that doesn't look as if it has been driven for a while, walk ahead on foot at first to ensure that you can get through. If you can't, report it to the council and find somewhere else to drive.

It is worth noting that most Rights of Way Offices are only open for a certain number of hours per week, so you should always telephone ahead and book an appointment. Most

*Fig.129 You should obey TRO notices like this one at all times.*

offices have a limited number of staff, so don't be disappointed if they can't accommodate you for as long as you would like. Allow plenty of time to mark up your maps, but don't overstay your welcome!

By putting time and effort into researching rights of way yourself, you are not only ensuring that the tracks you drive are 100 per cent legal, you will also find the driving of ancient roads and age-old vehicular rights of way much more enjoyable.

## OFF-ROADING ON 'GREEN LANES'

### TROs and VROs

As explained above, the most important part of driving a right of way or 'green lane' is ensuring that you do indeed have a 'right' to be there at the wheel of a 4x4 vehicle. Never assume that because there are some fresh tyre marks on a track that you too have a right to drive it. The tracks could belong to the landowner, farmer or the emergency services using the track as an access road. Recreational off-roaders may have no business being there, and you should always check the definitive map as discussed earlier to ensure that a BOAT or RUPP is 100 per cent legal.

Even legal BOATs and RUPPs may be subject to seasonal variations or temporary closure should the council believe them to be damaged or dangerous to users. Such restrictions are known as Traffic Regulation Orders, and any off-roader caught disobeying these legal notices is effectively breaking the law and may be subject to prosecution. Most

*Fig.130 Some byways are subject to seasonal restrictions, and these will always be clearly signposted.*

*Fig.131 Always stick to the proper route, even if that may not always be clear.*

TROs are well signposted at the start of the tracks, and the definitive map will also list them as being shut to traffic.

A different type of restriction notice has been developed by pro-land access bodies such as LARA (Land Access and Recreation Association) and GLASS (Green Lane ASSociation), which – although it has no legal status – should be observed by the recreational off-roader. Known as a Voluntary Restraint Order (VRO), a notice is placed at the start of a track urging people not to use it to prevent further damage being caused. The temporary suspension of use will allow the land to 'recover', thus preserving it for future use.

Some councils use such seasonal opening to allow well-used tracks to recover. The Gap Road in Wales for example is subject to a seasonal TRO which has been in force since late 1995. A sign at the end of the route tells users the dates when it can and cannot be driven, and anyone doing so outside these dates is breaking the law.

## Respect the Terrain

Once you have established that you are legally allowed to be on a specific track, second on the list of priorities is respect for the land – remember that although the track you are driving is a right of way, the land surrounding it is owned and/or used by someone, and you should treat it with the respect it deserves.

If you encounter a farmer or landowner on your travels and he questions the legality of the track, show him your map and explain that you have visited the Rights of Way Office and believe it to be a right of way. If he insists that he is right and that you have no business being there, turn around and go back the way you came, making a note to check the suspect area with County Hall as soon as possible. If the track is indeed a right of way then the farmer has no business to stop you, but discretion is always better than confrontation in these circumstances.

At all times stick to the track, making sure that you are still following the correct route by periodically checking your map. Quite often while off-roading you will come across other tracks that may not be marked on the map. These will often be routes to farms or tracks used by the landowner and you have no right to use them. Be careful also when there appear to be two routes leading to the same place. Sometimes these have been cut to avoid an obstacle that is blocking the track, and you will have to use common sense to pick the right one. If your choice turns out to be the wrong one, make a U-turn as soon as possible and get back on the right track. Never be tempted to make your own route or take a shortcut, as once again, you are effectively trespassing as soon as you leave the proper route.

When off-roading on a public right of way you should be aware that there will be other off-roaders, walkers, bikers and horse riders

*Fig.132 Always leave gates as you found them.*

*Fig.133 Some byways aren't suitable for newer vehicles – if you want to avoid getting your paintwork scratched that is!*

using the same route, and you should be polite and courteous at all times. As you are off-roading in a wheeled vehicle, you should give way to all other users, most notably walkers and horse riders. If you see one coming towards you, pull off the track, switch off your engine and let them pass. Once they are past, do not roar your engine and make off at top speed, instead gently carry on your way – any display of bad manners or bravado will tarnish the reputation of other users.

As you would if you were walking, follow the country code at all times. Leave gates as you found them, do not make excessive noise and tread lightly. The ideal off-road trip

would leave no trace of you ever having been there.

## Suitability of Routes

The existence of a right of way on the definitive map doesn't necessarily mean that it is suitable for all types of off-road vehicle. An overgrown lane that you might be prepared to take a battered old Land Rover down might prove too much for the owner of a brand new Range Rover as the foliage scrapes the highly polished paintwork!

Of course, there is no way of telling the

*Fig.134 Always be prepared for the unexpected when off-roading.*

severity of a byway that you haven't driven before, and it is up to you whether or not you drive it. A track that starts off relatively easily may suddenly become very difficult to traverse without the aid of a winch or at least with some appropriately aggressive off-road tyres. If at any stage the track starts to look more difficult than you imagined, turn around and find somewhere else to drive. Apart from damaging your vehicle, a long winching session may cause unnecessary damage to the ground.

On this note, some lanes may need to be treated with sensitivity, especially ones that are badly drained. Driving a vehicle along a waterlogged lane can cause serious damage to the terrain, with the resulting ruts forming

a channel for water to erode further. This type of lane should only be used in dry weather, where the environmental impact will be minimal.

## Hazards and Blockages

If you are travelling along a right of way in a wooded area you are likely to come across fallen trees or branches. If they are blocking the track and preventing you from continuing, you are perfectly at rights to winch the tree to one side, although you should never cut down live trees or deviate from the route to get through. Mud and boulders can also block the way ahead after particularly heavy rain, and again you should be sensitive to the environmental impact of any attempt to get past.

Some farmers and landowners have been known to lock gates on what are perfectly legal rights of way. Although this action is illegal, it is not advisable to cut the lock and drive on – instead give up on that particular route, turn around and notify the local council's Highways Department. They should be able to exercise some authority and get the gate unlocked.

If a byway is inadequately drained you will frequently come across seemingly innocuous looking puddles as you make your way along it. However with water erosion and heavy rain, these can often prove deeper than they appear. If you are in doubt, check the depth with a stick as discussed in Chapter 4 and only proceed if you are sure that it is safe to do so. By law the local council is responsible for ensuring that the lanes are possible to drive and kept in good condition. However, tumbling budgets mean that councils can't do as much as is required, so there are often green lane days where enthusiasts help keep the lanes in good order. If you hear of one in your local area try to go along to help out – as users we all have a part to play in ensuring that byways remain open.

## Be Prepared

You should always be prepared for the worst when off-roading – even though you are travelling on home turf, anything can happen. This is particularly important when you are off-roading in the more remote moorland areas where the nearest habitation may be as far as 15 miles away. Say the worst happened and you managed to roll your vehicle miles from anywhere and in the accident your passenger broke their arm. Ask yourself what you would do. Would you have the equipment to be able to rescue yourself,

and what would you do about that arm?

Although the above is unlikely, we cannot stress enough the importance of good preparation before you go off-roading. Be prepared for all weather conditions, especially sudden changes of temperature or the onset of rain. Take enough food with you to last for at least 24 hours, and a warm sleeping bag might be something worth considering if you plan to do a lot of miles in one day. A change of clothing is also worthwhile and if you have a mobile phone, take that as well. If there is service it can be a useful contact with the outside world.

If you are off-roading alone (something that we don't recommend) you should carry spares for all eventualities. If you break down and don't have the means to repair the vehicle, what alternative is there but to summon help or walk back?

One final piece of equipment that is useful is a CB radio. While in convoy, the CB can be used to keep in contact with your fellow 'laners', also to communicate during snatch recoveries or to offer 'helpful' advice on a tricky section that you have just driven.

## PRIVATE SITES AROUND THE UK AND OFF-ROAD DRIVING SCHOOLS

If playing in mud is your thing, where you enjoy nothing more than pointing your vehicle at the nearest mud hole and spending the next couple of hours winching it free, then you should avoid driving on rights of way at all costs. Driving and winching through mud can cause significant damage to the land, and whereas this is of little concern on private sites, churning up rights of way is both inconsiderate and irresponsible.

Fortunately there are a large number of well organized 'play days' held on private land to cater for the serious mud enthusiast,

*Fig.135 Playing in the mud should be restricted to private sites only, like this one here in Wales.*

*Fig.136 Speed and endurance are the keys to success in the competitive world of off-road motorsport.*

mostly organized by clubs or off-road centres. For the competitive driver, a regular series of competitive trials are available, ranging from the technical 'driving around canes' type to competitive safaris or hill rallies, where speed and endurance are the key to success. For a list of events contact a body like the All Wheel Drive Club or the Association of Rover Clubs, both of which are listed under Useful Addresses.

For the novice we recommend taking part in a day's training at one of the UK's many off-road driving schools. Although this book has covered most of the necessary techniques for successful and safe off-roading, you can't beat the hands-on experience given by the majority of off-road schools in the UK. A selected list of these is reproduced under Useful Addresses.

## OFF-ROADING ABROAD

As your experience and capability off-road increases so too might your desire for something different. Off-roading abroad can give you a vast range of experiences of driving on terrain that is simply not available in the UK. From breathtaking scenery to the sheer adventure of driving on foreign soil, there is much to recommend broadening your off-road horizons. After all, didn't you buy a 4x4 for adventure and its 'go anywhere' ability?

### Where To Go: Europe

Like the UK, in Europe you cannot just pull off the tarmac and drive wherever you want. Indeed, the rest of Europe has a variety of different laws regarding off-road driving: some countries have a *laissez-faire* attitude, while others have introduced draconian measures in order to prevent it.

France, for example, tried to ban recre-

ational off-roading in the late 1980s with the infamous *Loi Lalonde*, named after the vociferous MP that brought the bill into parliament. However, after several years of discussion, it seems as though it is now possible to drive off-road in most parts of France, although the local authorities have the power to close certain tracks through decrees issued by the *Mairie* or town hall. Most of these will be well signposted, but it is still prudent to ask permission from the *Mairie* if you want to drive a specific track.

By far the best way to explore the off-road tracks of France, however, is through one of

*Fig.137 France offers a number of superbly organized 'raids', and 'foreign' entries are welcome.*

the superbly organized 'raids' that take place throughout the year. Consisting of up to 200 vehicles, these make use of a rally-style roadbook to guide participants through some of the most beautiful scenery in France. As well as offering technically challenging off-roading, the sheer good-natured atmosphere and *joie de vivre* offered by these events make them ever popular amongst British off-road enthusiasts. Contact David Davenport and his company Long Range Off-Roading for further details.

Elsewhere in Europe things are a little more difficult. In Belgium the *Loi Wallonne* prohibits the driving of any motorized vehicle on forest tracks (with the notable exception of foresters and hunters), and as the remaining land is used for farming the situation is rather delicate. In Germany, Austria, Switzerland and the Netherlands the situation is worse. Put simply, any type of recreational off-roading is *verboten* unless you have express permission, which is almost always impossible to obtain. Italy frowns upon off-roading in the north, while it seems to be accepted in the warmer southern regions

In Spain and Portugal the situation is slightly better. For years it was possible to drive any off-road track without fear of being stopped, but irresponsible use by locals has curtailed this recently. There are still some tracks that are open for use, but it is worthwhile checking with the local authority before you drive them as the Guardia will take a dim view of any foreigner caught where they shouldn't be. Once again, the best way to explore Spain's beautiful scenery is with an organized event, and there are several companies that offer the chance to do this.

Finally, in Greece it is possible to drive anywhere. All byways have free access and no-one will interfere or prohibit you from driving through their land, as long as you

seek their permission first and stick to the tracks.

## Where To Go: USA, Africa and Beyond

For the real adventurer, the huge potential of off-roading in the vast continents of Africa and America is not to be missed. However, such long-range trips require much forethought and a great deal of planning – especially if you intend taking your own vehicle. It is beyond the scope of this book to go into too much detail about the preparations you will need to make before

*Fig.138 Off-roading in the USA is a simply spectacular experience.*

attempting an expedition, although we give a rough outline below.

Basically speaking, before embarking on an off-road expedition in somewhere like Africa, you need to be 100 per cent sure of your route, your vehicle and your own ability to cope with the inevitable problems that will arise. Organizations such as the Foreign Office travel advice line will be able to advise you on possible safety problems and be able to answer questions about any political insecurities. The AA or RAC international travel service can advise on legal obligations, while the consulate service of the country's embassy should offer assistance with visas and in other bureaucratic areas.

Finally the Expedition Advisory Centre at the Royal Geographical Society in Kensington will also be able to offer advice and first-hand knowledge on the country you intend to visit.

Immerse yourself in books and maps covering the countries you intend to visit so that you are fully able to appreciate their culture and customs. There is no such thing as too much information, and most guidebooks are reasonably accurate. If you can, talk also to people who have already carried out similar expeditions – their own mistakes and experiences will most definitely be worth knowing about. For the less adventurous, there are several 4x4 tours available in

*Fig. 139 A great deal of preparation is required before venturing off to the wide open spaces of Africa or Australia.*

Africa, some of which allow you to take your own vehicle.

The situation in the USA on the other hand is comparatively straightforward, as most of the areas suitable for off-roading in that vast continent are federally owned, allowing unrestricted access to established rights of way. The US Forestry and Bureau of Land Management catalogue and maintain the majority of these tracks, and regional maps showing the trails you can drive are available at their many offices.

Once again it is perhaps preferable for the first time off-roader in the States to participate in one of the many 'official' off-road trips, the most slickly organized seeming to be the Jeepers Jamborees that run throughout the year. It goes without saying that these events are limited to Jeep vehicles only! A contact address for the Jeepers is listed in under Useful Addresses.

When off-roading in the USA, one of the main problems for the foreign off-roader is what vehicle to use. Whereas it is quite possible to temporarily import your own 4x4, the costs and bureaucracy involved are prohibitive unless you intend to spend several months off-roading. To overcome this, there are a number of 4x4 hire companies that – in the main – offer well-prepared Jeeps for use both on and off-road. There may be one or two restrictions on the trails you can drive, but for the most part this is comparable with having your own vehicle. Wherever you travel, the experiences that a 4x4 vehicle can offer simply cannot be beaten.

*Fig.140 Jeep hire for off-road use is widely available in America.*

# Useful Addresses

## Off-Road Vehicle Manufacturers and Importers

Chrysler/Jeep UK,
Poulton Close,
Dover,
CT17 0HP
Tel: 01304 228877

Daihatsu UK,
Poulton Close,
Dover,
CT17 0HP
Tel: 01304 213030

Ford Motor Company,
Eagle Way,
Brentwood,
Essex,
CM13 3BW
Tel: 01277 253000

Isuzu,
International Motors Group Limited,
Ryder Street,
West Bromwich,
Midlands,
B70 0EJ
Tel: 0121 522 2000

Lada Cars,
3120 Park Square,
Birmingham Business Park,
Birmingham,
West Midlands,
B37 7YN
Tel: 0121 717 9000

Land Rover UK,
Lode Lane,
Solihull,
West Midlands,
B92 8NW
Tel: 0121 722 2424

Mitsubishi Motors,
The Colt Car Company Limited,
Watermoor,
Cirencester,
Glos.
GL7 1LF
Tel: 01285 755777

Nissan UK,
Rivers Office Park,
Maple Cross,
Rickmansworth,
Hertfordshire,
WD3 2YS
Tel: 01923 899933

Steyr-Puch Limited,
Unit 7 Lawson Hunt Industrial Park,
Guildford Road,
Broadbridge Heath,
Horsham,
RH12 3JR
Tel: 01403 211976

Suzuki UK,
46–62 Gatwick Road,
Crawley,
West Sussex,
RH10 2XF
Tel: 01293 518000

Toyota Motors GB,
The Quadrangle,
Redhill,
Surrey,
Tel: 01737 768585

Vauxhall Motor Company,
Griffin House,
Luton,
Bedfordshire,
LU1 3YT
Tel: 01582 21122

## Off-Road Equipment Suppliers/Vehicle Preparation

Action-Mobil,
Leogandgerstr. 53,
A-5760,
Saalfelden,
Austria
*Camper conversions for off-road expeditions.*

ADI Engineering,
4B Heron Business Park,
Whitefield Avenue,
Luton,
LU3 3BB
Tel: 01582 563663
Fax: 01582 563669
*Off-road vehicle preparation. Specialists in off-road racing.*

AJS 4x4 Services,
Kingswood Knoll,
Brighton Road,
Lower Kingswood,
Surrey,
KT20 6XN
Tel: 01737 241370
Fax: 01737 246073
*Off-road tyres and vehicle preparation.*

Automatic Conversions,
133 Victoria Street,
Dunstable,
Bedfordshire,
LU6 3BB
Tel: 01582 477680
Fax: 01582 477030
*Suppliers of Detroit locking differentials.*

Drew Bowler Off-Road Motorsport,
Over Lane Farm,
Hazelwood,
Derbyshire,
DE56 4AG
Tel: 01773 550324
Fax: 01773 550074
*Specialist roll cage manufacturer and off-road motorsport preparation.*

David Bowyer's Off-Road Centre,
East Foldhay,
Zeal Monachorum,
Devon,
EX17 6LR
Tel: 01363 82666
Fax: 01363 82782
*Supplier of off-road recovery equipment, including Superwinch winches and fitting kits.*

Bushey Hall Limited,
Unit 7 Lismarrane Industrial Park,
Elstree Road
Elstree,
Hertfordshire,
WD6 3EE
Tel: 0181 953 6050
Fax: 0181 207 5308
*Winch manufacturer and equipment supplier.*

Caranex,
Cuan Ferry,
Seil,
Oban,
Argyll,
PA34 4RB
Tel: 01852 300258
*Manufacturers of the vehicle-mounted Caranex tent.*

John Craddock Limited,
70–76 North Street,
Bridgtown,
Cannock,
Staffordshire,
WS11 3AZ
Tel: 01543 577207
Fax: 01543 504818
*Off-road tyres and equipment.*

Dixon Bate,
Unit 45 Deeside Industrial Park,
Deeside,
Clwyd,
CH5 2LG
Tel: 01244 288925
Fax: 01244 288462
*Manufacturers of recovery and towing accessories.*

KAM Differentials Limited,
Clock Barn House,
Hambledon Road,
Godalming,
Surrey,
GU8 4AY
Tel: 01483 419779
Fax: 01483 417558
*Suppliers of heavy-duty transmission components.*

Mantec Services (UK),
Unit One, The Green,
Hartshill,
Nuneaton,
CV10 0FW
Tel/fax: 01203 395368
*Expedition preparation and suppliers of the Mantec snorkel.*

New Concept,
PO Box 61,
Winchester,
SO23 8XR
Tel: 01962 865996
*Distributor for the Easy Lift exhaust air jack.*

ORCA Off-Road Equipment,
Hinton Lodge,
Hinton,
Saxmundham,
Suffolk,
IP17 3HG
Tel: 01508 478000
Fax: 01508 478001
*Supplier of ORCA ground anchors and bridging ladders.*

Ryders International,
Knowsley Road,
Bootle,
Liverpool,
L20 4NW
Tel: 0151 922 7585
Fax: 0151 944 1424
*Sole UK importer for Warn winches.*

Safety Devices,
Regal Drive,
Soham,
Cambridge,
CB7 5BE
Tel/Fax: 01353 624624
*Manufacturer of underside protection and roll cages.*

Simmonites,
755 Thornton Road,
Thornton,
Bradford,
West Yorkshire
Tel: 01274 833351
Fax: 01274 835117
*Suppliers of tyres and off-road equipment.*
*Manufacturers of Simmbugghini off-road*
*racers.*

Sinton Tyres,
Unit 15 Broughton Manor Park,
Milton Keynes,
Bucks,
MK16 0HF
Tel: 01908 665591
Fax: 01908 604667
*Off-road tyres.*

Southdown 4x4 Products,
Southdown,
Zeal Monachorum,
Devon,
EX17 6DR
Tel: 01363 83819
Fax: 01363 83472
*Manufacturer of off-road protection accessories.*

Superwinch Limited,
South Station Yard,
Abbey Rise,
Tavistock,
Devon,
PL19 9BS
Tel: 01822 614101
*Manufacturer of Superwinch winches.*

Surrey Off-Road,
Alford Road,
Dunsfold,
Surrey,
Tel: 01483 200046
Fax: 01483 200047
*Agent for Old Man Emu suspension and ARB*
*equipment. Vehicle preparation.*

Terratrip UK Limited,
Ship Farm,
Horsley,
Derby,
DE2 5BR
Tel/Fax: 01332 882640
*Suppliers of the Terratrip rally/trip*
*computers.*

Thule,
Bourne Enterprise Centre,
Borough Green,
Kent,
TN15 8DG
*Suppliers of Thule roof boxes.*

UK Wire and Rope,
15 Ronald Rolph Court,
Wadloes Road,
Cambridge,
CB5 8PX
Tel: 01223 414361
Fax: 01223 416657
*Off-road recovery equipment.*

## Off-Road Driving Schools

David Bowyer's Off-Road Centre,
East Foldhay,
Zeal Monachorum,
Devon,
EX17 6LR
Tel: 01363 82666
Fax: 01363 82782

John Cockburn Off-Road,
Murryshill,
Cambusbarron,
Stirling,
FK7 9QA
Tel: 01786 448356
Fax: 01786 446455

Fresh Tracks
Haultwick Farm,
Ware,
Hertfordshire,
SL11 1JQ
Tel: 01920 438758
Fax: 01920 438729

Golding Barn 4x4 Off-Road Driving Centre,
64 Roman Road,
Steyning,
Sussex,
BN44 3FN
Tel/fax: 01903 812195

Landcraft,
Plas-yn-Dre,
High Street,
Bala,
Gwynedd,
LL23 7LU
Tel: 01678 520820
Fax: 01678 520152

Lakeland Safari,
Duddon View,
9 Castlewray,
Broughton in Furness,
Cumbria,
LA20 6EW
Tel/fax: 01229 716943

The Land Rover Experience,
Lode Lane,
Solihull,
B92 8NW
Tel: 0121 722 2424

Off-Road London,
PO Box 4776,
London,
SE2 0YZ
Tel: 0181 265 3760

Pink Elephant Off the Road,
The Old Stable Yard,
Duke of Somerset's Estate,
Maiden Bradley,
Wiltshire,
BA12 7HL
Tel: 01985 844844

Pro-Trax,
32 Southfield,
Gretton,
Corby,
Northamptonshire,
NN17 3BX
Tel/fax: 01536 770096

Ronnie Dale Off-Road,
Whiteburn Farm,
Abbey St Bathans,
Duns,
Berwickshire,
TD11 3RU
Tel: 01361 840244
Fax: 01361 840239

Tuf-Trax,
Westerings,
Station Road,
West Haddon,
Northamptonshire,
NN6 7AU
Tel: 01788 510575
Fax: 01788 510227

Wild Tracks,
Chippenham Road,
Kennett,
Newmarket,
Suffolk,
CB8 7QJ
Tel: 01638 751918
Fax: 01638 552173

Yorkshire 4x4 Explorations,
The Green Dragon Inn,
Exelby,
North Yorkshire,
DL8 2HA
Tel: 01677 427222
Fax: 01677 427333

## Clubs

All Wheel Drive Club,
PO Box 6,
Fleet,
Hants,
GU13 9YE

Association of Rover Clubs,
14 Bolton Road,
Rochdale,
Lancashire,
OL11 4BP
Tel: 01706 38801
*Will be able to supply details of your local
Land Rover club.*

Club Discovery,
West Farm,
Witham on the Hill,
Bourne,
Lincolnshire,
PE10 0JN
Tel: 01778 590500

Fox All Wheel Drive Club,
37 Rosedale Gardens,
Thatcham,
Newbury,
Berkshire,
RG19 3LE
Tel: 01635 868875

Isle of Wight 4x4 Club,
75 Church Road,
Wootton,
Isle of Wight,
PO33 4PZ
Tel: 01983 882381

Lutterworth Overlanders,
71 Woodmarket,
Lutterworth,
Leicestershire,
LE17 4BI

Scottish Off-Road Club,
1 Hallyard Farm Cottages,
Kirkliston,
EH29 9DZ
Tel: 0131 333 4291
Fax: 0131 333 4600

Suffolk 4WD Club,
9 Otago Close,
Whittlesey,
Peterborough,
PE7 1YL
Tel: 01733 202746

West Wales 4x4 Group,
Trenaa,
Beulah,
Newcastle Emlyn,
Dyfed,
SA38 9QB
Tel: 01239 810050

## Miscellaneous

The African Interior Safari Company,
PO Box 12222,
Edinburgh,
EH4 1YY
Tel/Fax: 0131 332 1101

The British Library Map Room,
Great Russell Street,
London,
WC1B 3DG
Tel: 0171 636 1544

Bureau of Land Management (USA),
Eastern States Office,
Department FW,
350 S. Pickett Street,
Alexandria,
VA 22304
USA

The Green Lane Association (GLASS)
9 Ffordd y Dderwen,
Llangewydd Court,
Bridgend,
Mid Glamorgan,
CF31 4TQ
Tel: 01656 767264

International Off-Roader Magazine,
120 Queen's Road,
Bury St Edmunds,
Suffolk,
IP33 3ES
Tel: 01284 752340
Fax: 01284 752343

Jeep Jamboree Headquarters
12755 State Highway 55
Minneapolis
MN 55441–8284
USA

Land Rover Owner Magazine,
Anglian House,
Chapel Lane,
Botesdale,
Norfolk,
IP22 1DT
Tel: 01379 890056

Long Range Off-Roading,
Copseland,
Woodland Avenue,
Cranleigh,
Surrey,
GU6 7HU
Tel/Fax: 01483 273786
*Agent for organized off-road events and 'raids' in France and Europe.*

The Map Shop,
15 High Street,
Upton upon Severn,
Worcestershire,
WR8 0JH
Tel: 01684 593146
Fax: 01684 594559
*Map suppliers, both national and international.*

Medical Advisory Service for Travellers Abroad,
c/o London School of Hygiene and Tropical Medicine,
Keppel Street,
London,
WC1E 7HT
Tel: 0171 631 4408
Fax: 0171 436 5389

Ordnance Survey,
Romsey Road,
Maybush,
Southampton,
SO9 4DH
Tel: 01703 792000

Pumkin Marine and Leisure Limited,
100 The Highway,
London,
E1 9BX
Tel: 0171 480 6630
Fax: 0171 481 8905
*Suppliers of GPS and VHF radio equipment.*

The Royal Geographical Society,
1 Kensington Gore,
London,
SW7 2AR
Tel: 0171 589 5466
Fax: 0171 584 4447

K & J Slavin (Quest) Limited,
Cow Pasture Farm,
Louth Road,
Hainton,
Lincoln,
LN3 6LX
Tel: 01507 313401
Fax: 01507 313609
*Expedition preparation and consultancy service.*

Stanfords,
12–14 Long Acre,
Covent Garden,
London,
WC2E 9LP
Tel: 0171 836 1321
Fax: 0171 836 0189
*World maps by mail order.*

Trailmasters,
45 King Street,
West Malling,
Kent,
ME19 6QT
Tel: 01732 870184
Fax: 01732 845503
*Expedition organizer for Africa and Eastern Europe. Equipment supplier.*

# Index